FOOTBALL, FLYING & FAITH

"AIM HIGH"

FOOTBALL, FLYING & FAITH

DICK ABEL | BRIG. GEN. RET.

Foreword by Chad Hennings
Former Dallas Cowboys and Air Force Academy Falcons

ISBN: 978-1-948282-44-4
Football, Flying & Faith

Football, Flying & Faith is registered with the Library of Congress.

For permission requests, write to the publisher at the address below:
Yorkshire Publishing
3207 South Norwood Avenue
Tulsa, Oklahoma 74135
www.YorkshirePublishing.com
918.394.2665

Dedication

Where does one begin when writing a dedication for a book that covers a lifetime? After prayer, counsel, and with God's inspiration, I dedicate my story to all the people who have had an influence in my life. Pastors, teachers, leaders, athletes, neighbors, friends, and military associates, all have shaped my life. I'm very thankful for each one and honored to broadly recognize all, whether by name or in my recollections.

There is one group that affected me in a profound way, and that is the first Radford High School Fellowship of Christian Athletes Huddle in Hawaii, founded in 1970. The original twelve guys were student athletes, mainly basketball players. These boys set a spiritual course for their school as well as others on Oahu. Five of these 1972 graduates went on to Service Academies. Two of "our boys" from this group, Commander Andy Tamayo and Colonel Gary Lorenzen, have gone before us to heaven. Many are now in full-time Christian ministry. We lovingly dedicate this book to them.

Acknowledgment

This book is the result of a team of gifted people. Under God's direction, they have captured the life of an ordinary man, who is humbled by their efforts. Rita Tate is a talented cowriter. Dr. Richard Tate has had his "hand on the stick" guiding us along, and my beloved Miss Ann is an invaluable editor. To all the Tate Publishing teams who have contributed...well done! Collectively this has been an *all-star* performance. A thousand thanks for your combined efforts.

Contents

Foreword

When I think of Dick Abel, I think of a *renaissance man*. His is a life that has transcended athletics—college athlete, coach, and senior leader of the United States Olympic Committee; military service, pilot, public affairs officer assisting with the repatriation of our Vietnam Prisoners of War, Director of Public Affairs for Office of Secretary of the Air Force, and retired general officer; and Christian missions, President of Fellowship of Christian Athletes and Director of Military Ministry for Campus Crusade for Christ. Everything in his life has exemplified servant leadership. He has impacted the lives of so many men, including myself, to live a life of integrity, excellence, and spiritual purpose.

I first met Brigadier General Abel while I was a young cadet at the Air Force Academy. I was trying to find my way as a student athlete and budding Air Force officer. When Coach Abel introduced himself, I was intimidated by the rank because when an officer would speak to an underclassman, it would many times send shivers up and down the inexperienced cadet's spine. But Coach Abel was different. The wisdom and compassion he exuded instilled confidence in those with whom he came in contact—me included. Then, as the years passed, I began to see the man of faith and purpose. General Abel lives purposefully by being a servant leader and encouraging everyone he influenced to live a life of transformation for Christ. He is a man I strive to be like and someone I hold up as a role model for my son.

Football, Flying & Faith! is the story of General Abel's remarkable life and a book that you will enjoy and want to share with any young person who is looking to find their own purpose in life.

Chad Hennings
USAFA Class of 1988
A-10 Pilot
Three-Time NFL Super Bowl Champion with the Dallas Cowboys

Introduction

I thank God every day that I am still in the game—the game of life. In fact, even at my age, I'm still learning the fundamentals essential to the game. Wasn't it yesterday I was catching that pass or blocking for a teammate on a muddy football field as a youngster at St. Ignatius High School in Cleveland, Ohio? It seems only days ago when I strapped into a T-34 and took off for my first solo flight. The memories come flooding back—marrying the "Yellow Rose of Texas," children born, coaching, instructing young men, serving in Vietnam, working with navy admirals, being assigned to the Pentagon, becoming a general officer, retiring, and then serving on the US Olympic Committee's senior staff, heading the Fellowship of Christian Athletes and, later, the Military Ministry of Campus Crusade for Christ—it all happened in a blink. So did becoming a grandfather and great-grandfather. One could say the subtitle for this book "Aim High" fits my life.

Within the small capsule of time, that totals more than eighty years I have had unique privileges afforded to very few. Perhaps that is why many friends and family members have encouraged me to document and share some of these experiences and events in this book, *Football, Flying & Faith!* I know any accomplishments credited to me have been the result of others, including my family, who thought more of me than I deserved. At critical points of my life, they believed in me, encouraged me, and taught me to live with vision and purpose. Theirs are strong shoulders upon which I stand. Most of all, I am eternally grateful to my Lord and Savior Jesus Christ. Through His grace, I've been redeemed and His "mercies are new to me every morning" (Lamentations 3:22–23).

Putting the Lord first in my life has given me the strength, confidence, skills and the faith I needed to make tough decisions and to help others achieve their own goals. I was taught early in my life that common sense and hard work is critical to success; however, true wisdom only comes from God. Because God has been the center of my life, I pray I have been a better leader, as well as husband, father, and grandfather, and a better man.

The phases of my life are evident in the three words making up the title of this book. What do the words *football*, *flying*, and *faith* have in common? Each discipline suggests a point of determination, choice, and commitment. A football player works hard and pays the price to make the team, a pilot commits to learning in order to be an accomplished flyer, and a believer makes a conscious decision to follow Christ in every area of life. Through these pages of my life, I hope readers make or renew their own commitment to God's plan for their lives. After all, life is a game that no one wants to lose.

~ 1 ~

A Kid from Detroit

There is still a slight chill in the air as I sit on the back porch of our home in Poquoson, part of Hampton Roads, Virginia. I hear Ann stirring in the kitchen, clearing our breakfast plates from the table, and take notice that none of the trees in the backyard are budding. The calendar says it is spring, but winter seems reluctant to go. Soon the green will return, and Ann will be busy planting, tending, puttering around in the yard as usual. I can't help but reflect on the changing seasons of my own life too. Hopefully, I have a few more left before the final one because I have much left to do. That is the way it has always been. I live for one more challenge, one more project, and one more opportunity to make a difference. That little kid who grew up on West 57th Street in Cleveland could never have envisioned the wonderful life I have lived. This is how it started...

The world was listening to the stirrings of upcoming war when I was born on October 28, 1933, in Akron, Ohio, to Cecelia and Frank Abel. Adolph Hitler had been appointed the chancellor of Germany earlier that year and newly elected president of the United States, Franklin D. Roosevelt, introduced the New Deal legislation to help get America's workers back on track during the Great Depression. I arrived in the middle of the Depression while my parents, like most of the country, struggled to make ends meet. Through the years, my mother would proudly state we never had to join the welfare rolls; our family somehow made it through without government assistance. Soon after my birth, the family, which included my older sister, Joan, now deceased, moved to Cleveland's west side to live with my grandparents. Nine years later, our younger brother Frank was born.

I came from hardy German stock, grandparents who were hardworking, devout European/German Roman Catholics, who immigrated from Germany, entering the country through Ellis Island and settling in the Cleveland area. Staunchly true to the Catholic faith, they raised their four children to be "good Catholics." In fact, Grandfather, Mike Kleinhenz, was a janitor and caretaker of the local Catholic church. My father was the oldest of the four Abel children, a fact which became extremely relevant when his father was hit by a streetcar and died from his injuries. Dad was only sixteen years old. At that time, he was attending St. Ignatius, a Catholic high school, but had to quit school in order to help provide monetarily for his mother and siblings.

Dad met mother, and they married in 1930. After my sister and I were born, he took a job in Pittsburg, and we moved there for six months, then returned to settle in Rocky River, Ohio, a western suburb of Cleveland. By this time, Dad had become trained to be a refrigeration serviceman, a growing need as that technology developed. He was soon able to open his own small appliance store and office in Rocky River, and Mom took care of the books. Because Dad was flat-footed, he was not able to serve in World War II but worked for a time in a tank factory in Cleveland. By the time America joined the war effort in 1941, I was only ten years old but already helping out at our store, Suburban Appliance. We were not wealthy by any means, but I never thought we were poor; our needs were met. We had food, clothing, and shelter and a strong family unit.

I grew up learning three important things from my father: First, he was a people person, a caring man genuinely interested in others. He spent hours visiting with customers, neighbors, friends. So much so, Mom would comment, "It is a wonder your Dad gets any work done." Secondly, Dad was a man of integrity. "Your word is your bond," he would say. He also encouraged me, "Finish what you start, no matter how difficult it is." Then, thirdly, he championed hard work. "Do the best you can and work hard." Those were Dad's simple keys to success, and they have served me well over the years.

Mom was the main disciplinarian in our home, but Dad could get really riled if we dared talk back or sass Mother in any way. I once received a distinct thump to the side of my head after I made some offhand remark to my mom.

I was an active kid who enjoyed sports from a young age. Along with neighborhood pickup games, I played team basketball and football in addition to catching for American Legion baseball during the summer breaks. I recall that Geigers, a local haberdashery store, paid for our baseball uniforms. Later, at St. Ignatius High School (the same Catholic high school Dad attended), I did a little boxing, enough to get my nose broken, but began to concentrate more on football. I was an end for the team and simply loved the game.

The Ignatius High School Wildcats were good; we would win the city championship while I was there. In fact, nine guys were given partial or full scholarships to college out of that team, and I was one of them. Many Ignatius boys, then and now, are recruited especially by Notre Dame every year. The athletic director while I was there was Father Bill Sullivan who greatly influenced me and others. Years later, I would bring my son along for a visit to Cleveland, and we stopped by to see Father Sullivan who had retired. He was telling my son, Tim, how great I was as a student and athlete. Well, I actually was not a great student, but I was recruited by eight colleges. I'm proud of my alma mater—the school continues to produce outstanding student athletes year after year.

My partial scholarship to the University of Detroit, Michigan's largest Catholic university, was granted with the condition that I would make the team in the fall. The team doctor for the Titans also served as the track coach. He convinced me that I needed to work on my running ability in order to make the team and keep the scholarship. I ran pretty well, or so I thought, a 10 flat 100. However, put up against the other excellent athletes, I came in sixth! Still, thankfully, the football coach said, "Abel, you are the last one of the guys we are going to keep," and my scholarship was extended. Many players out of that team would receive offers to play professional football, miraculously, even me.

I had to work while in college, but that was nothing new. I had worked in some capacity since I was twelve years old. My first job was delivering newspapers, which meant rising early to throw the route no matter the weather, then collecting money from customers, tough work for a kid. I also worked at a gas station, a hardware store, and a drug store, but mostly worked for my dad at his appliance store.

In college, I had a wide variety of jobs—dug ditches at one time, delivered ice, and worked as a bookkeeper. I dug ditches for the sewer system at the Ford plant across from the Cleveland airport. Man, that was back-breaking work. Once, a big bruiser digging along side me said, "Hey, boy, you're working too fast. Slow down. You are going to work us out of a job!" I think I made close to $1 an hour, but if I was picked to work on Saturdays, I made double the pay. I also worked as a maître d' at an Italian restaurant, a bookkeeper for a dress shop, and an accountant for an auto repair business.

Probably the worst college job I recall was painting the trim on windows at a convent in Cleveland in the summer. The nuns were wonderful to offer me refreshment during those hot, sweltering days. They would bring me lemonade and cookies, but it was the most tedious job ever; the hours seemed to crawl by.

One particular college job would have a lasting impact. I worked for a time as an "ice man." We delivered ice to homes, stores, breweries, and theaters. One day, as I pulled a 350-pound block of ice out of the storage area, I slipped and hit my head on a glass chute resulting in a serious concussion. In fact, bystanders said I shouldn't have survived, the impact was that intense. This injury would have a problematic effect on my life in the coming years.

I was on the brink of adulthood but never wavered from my Catholic upbringing. It defined who I was. I grew up like all good Catholics, attending mass every Sunday, going to confession, did "Hail Marys," prayed, and followed the traditions I'd been taught. To this day, I am grateful for the foundation of faith that my parents instilled in me. We even had an altar in our home, and I never doubted there was a God who loved me. I also knew about the sacrifice Jesus made on the cross and believed He died to save me.

There would come a point later in my life when that spiritual knowledge from strong Catholic roots would make its way from my head to my heart, and I would come to walk in an intimacy with Christ I never knew possible. But that was several years later.

~ 2 ~

My First Loves—Football, Flying and Ann

I enjoyed my college years at the University of Detroit where I continued to play football and run track and did both pretty well. So well in fact, by the time I finished my junior year, I had been contacted by four professional football teams. I had played several positions, including being a place kicker. I even received helpful pointers from one of the best. Some older readers may remember the name of Lou Groza, an Ohio boy who went on to set NFL records for place kicking. Nicknamed "The Toe," Groza played his entire career for the Cleveland Browns and was responsible for making place kicking part of specialized play.

I met Lou while shagging balls for him and quarterback Otto Graham before the start of the Browns preseason camp in 1953 and 1954. Groza retired in 1959 and was later named to the National Football League Hall of Fame in 1974. He passed away at the age of seventy-six in 2000. He made a huge impression on me as a young college athlete, and I began to believe I could possibly have a career playing professional football.

It was not to be. I returned to the University of Detroit as a college senior excited and hopeful, only to "blow out" a shoulder at the beginning of the year in one of our first games, dashing my dreams of an NFL career. Having been on a full ride scholarship for three years, the university asked me to be a graduate assistant for the football team after my injury, so my tuition was paid through my senior year, and I was grateful for the help.

Realizing that professional football was no longer an option, I shifted my focus and graduated in January of 1956 with a bachelor of science degree in business administration and entered the Air Force in March of 1956 with a ROTC commission as a second lieutenant in the Air Force, on my way to becoming a pilot. I had known for a long time that I wanted to fly.

I didn't have many serious romantic relationships through high school. I dated a few girls in high school who attended our Catholic sister school, but they were mostly group dates, along with a gang of football buddies and their dates. Then, while in college, I met a young lady, and we quickly became engaged to be married. Her father worked for a Cadillac dealership, and to be honest, the thought of a new Cadillac now and then may have been part of the attraction. I never felt like she was totally on board with my choice to enter the Air Force after graduation, but I remained in the relationship while headed for preflight training at Lackland Air Force Base in San Antonio, Texas.

I had no way of knowing that I would soon meet the love of my life, my "Yellow Rose of Texas," Shirley Ann Voelcker (Ann), the girl who would become a lifelong partner. I will let Ann tell the story.

Ann ~

I met Dick on a blind date. That's right—sometimes they do work out. Dick jokes that it was indeed a *blind* date because I was *blind*, and he was my *date*. My girlfriend, Carolyn, had called me to say she had somehow wound up with two dates for a Friday night. They were with two flyboys from Lackland Air Force Base in San Antonio. To help her out, she was hoping I could go out on a double date to fix the problem. Dick's buddy, Gene Carlson, talked him into going on the date. I was in my first year of college at that time, but always the dutiful daughter, I asked Carolyn to talk to my father, a Texas rancher with old-fashioned values. Dad responded, "Only if the boy will come an hour early to meet and talk with me first. Then, I'll decide if you can go."

The fact that Dick was willing to agree to Daddy's condition for the date is somewhat of a miracle in itself, given that he had never even seen me. But he came to the house and spent an hour visiting with Daddy, and they had a casual, comfortable talk, while I was in the next room on pins and needles. Finally, Daddy came in and said, "Okay, you can go out with him, but you have to be in by eleven o'clock." Dick is convinced that Daddy liked him because his shoes were shined!

Dick and I had a nice time. When we got back to the house, we found Daddy waiting for us on the front porch. After Dick pulled away, Daddy, who was a man of few words, said, "Well, Little Bit [using his pet name for me], that's the man you are going to marry."

"Oh, Daddy, no, he's only here for six weeks. Then he'll be gone."

Following that first date, Dick called me nearly every day, and we began to see each other as often as possible. He and my father really hit it off. Daddy loved football, and he and Dick could talk for hours about the sport. Before I met Dick, I dated a basketball player, and we had just broken up days before. Otherwise, I wouldn't have considered going on the date.

At one point, I had considered leaving San Antonio and going away for college in Denton, Texas, but Dad wouldn't have it. "Little Bit, I want you to stay at home," he said, and I would never have gone against his wishes, so I attended a junior college in San Antonio. Looking back, I realize that I would never have met Dick if I had been in school somewhere far from home, and that was God's plan. Another part of the plan was Dick spraining an ankle playing intramural basketball, which resulted in him being held over to the next class, giving us more time together.

Dick and I were getting to know each other when he abruptly planned a trip back to Michigan. I didn't know at the time that he was actually engaged to a girl there. I would learn later the purpose of his trip was to break off the engagement with his fiancée. He thought it should be done face-to-face.

Dick left me his car while he was away, but Daddy wouldn't let me drive it, even though I had learned to drive on the ranch and had been driving since I was fourteen years old. Anyway, a mere twenty-four hours later, I got a call from Dick. "Can you come and pick me up at the airport?" he said.

"What are you doing back here?" I asked, surprised he was back so quickly. I don't recall his answer, but I went to pick him up, and our friendship grew quickly into a romantic relationship.

As Ann and I grew closer, I knew I was falling in love with the beautiful girl with the blonde pony tail and captivating smile. We dated regularly until I left for more initial pilot training in Tucson. When I returned on July 4, Ann's family were making vacation plans. The hardworking couple had never really taken a vacation because it was difficult to take time away from the ranch, but they finally agreed to a trip to California. Specifically they wanted to visit Los Angeles. Ann's younger brother, Louis, would go along as well. The family even bought a new Studebaker for the trip!

On the way to California, the family stopped in Tucson. Ann's father and I had agreed that this stopover would be the perfect time for me to propose. So while driving over to join a squadron bowling competition that I was part of, I asked Ann to marry me. Her response? "Well, I have to think about this."

I said, "You have an hour and a half in the bowling alley to think about it." I know, romantic, right?

After the bowling match, she made me a happy young man by saying *yes*.

Ann's mother, however, was less than enthusiastic about the idea. In fact, she was quite upset. "Ann, he is Catholic and a Yankee besides. You don't really know him or his family. What if insanity runs in the family?" Ann had been raised in the Presbyterian church but educated at a Catholic girl's high school, so I couldn't quite understand why her mother was so negative about the fact that I was Catholic.

After my proposal, the trip could not be salvaged. Mrs. Voelcker continued to be very upset, so they turned the Studebaker around and headed back to Texas. For the record, Ann's mother finally warmed up to the idea of having me as a son-in-law, and we had a great friendship over many years until she passed away at the age of one hundred in 2007. By the way, they never made that trip out west.

Ann and I were married in a Catholic ceremony on November 10, 1956, in the chapel at Fort Sam Houston, an Army base in San Antonio. We didn't have a huge wedding, mostly Ann's friends and family, because my family and friends were all back east. Even on our wedding day, Ann still had a few jitters about marriage; after all, she was barely nineteen-years-old, and we hadn't spent much time together. As her father walked her down the aisle, he could tell she was very nervous. "Daddy, I don't know if I can do this," she whispered.

"Oh, yes, you can." And he began to tell her a funny story from his childhood, which calmed her down. Folks in the audience thought it was very sweet that dad and daughter were talking all the way down the aisle to the front. I remain grateful for Mr. Voelcker's confidence in me. He assured Ann more than once, "Dick will always take good care of you." I have tried my best to always do just that.

After a three-day honeymoon, I reported to Laredo Air Force Base for further pilot training, receiving my wings in May of 1957. Ann was settling into life as a military wife and actually enjoying it. When she went to the base office to get her new identification card, she was filling out the paperwork when suddenly a man in uniform came through the door behind her. Everyone immediately stood up, came to attention, and saluted. Ann turned around, saw the man, and thought she'd better salute too. Turns out the officer was the base commander, Colonel Milton Adams. From then on, whenever she and the commander met, he'd salute her. It was their inside joke.

I was proud of Ann as she adapted to the Air Force. She was one of the youngest wives but made friends easily. Our home in Laredo was a small apartment with living room, kitchen, bedroom, and bath. It was part of an old hacienda that had been converted into six apartments. There were orange and grapefruit trees in the courtyard. Our little apartment was always open to the young bachelors from the base who needed a home-cooked meal now and then. We'd feed them, talk with them, and give them some semblance of home life.

Ten months after we married, we were blessed by the birth of our first daughter. Tamara Diann (middle name is a combination of Dick and Ann) was born on September 19, 1957. We would call her Tammy.

Ann, young and inexperienced, had a lot to learn about motherhood but caught on fast. She tells about a large, stout nurse bringing Tammy to her for the first time in the hospital. She took one look at Ann's long fingernails and said, "I'm not giving you this baby with those claws!" Then she handed Ann some surgical scissors and watched while Ann cut off her nails, which were her pride and joy. Ann said she then took the precious bundle in her arms and muttered, "Sweet little baby, I hope you know more about this thing than I do." We both had to do some on-the-job training as parents. We learned a lot with our firstborn.

At first, Ann seemed okay with establishing our family in the Catholic faith. Remember, when non-Catholics marry a Catholic, they sign a document promising to raise their children in Catholicism. It wasn't until Tammy was born that she began to question some of the tenets of the Catholic church. She honestly did not see how she could rear children in a faith in which she was not totally in agreement. I was born and raised a Catholic, and it was all I had ever known, so I couldn't quite understand her issues with the church. We had a lot to work out in that regard but knew we would find some kind of middle ground.

After pilot training and receiving my wings, I returned to Lackland Air Force Base in San Antonio as a training officer for aviation cadets. The new commander of Lackland was Major General Robert Stillman, who had been the first commandant at the Air Force Academy. When I learned he needed an aide, I didn't volunteer for the job because I didn't know what an aide was. However, as it turned out, he selected *me* for the job, so I became General Stillman's aide-de-camp as a lieutenant. The general would often say he chose me for his aide so I could organize the Lackland football team and the Warhawks Flying Demonstration Team. "He also aided me once in a while," the General would quip. I also became the general's pilot. It was a great job.

How do you explain a love for flying? It's among the most exhilarating, freeing, satisfying experiences one can have. Leonardo da Vinci is credited with this statement: "Once you have tasted flight, you will forever walk the earth with your eyes turned skyward, for there you have been, and there you will always long to return." I couldn't have said it better. For over a year and a half, I would have the privilege of leading and performing with a great flying team, the four-member crew of The Warhawks. The Air Force used to have a number of teams across the country, and it took a special pilot to be part of any acrobatic squad. I'll never forget how it felt as all four of us would take off in formation. The last one off the ground would call "gear up" for all of us; then, we'd come across the three-hundred-foot runway in a fingertip or diamond position, wing tips just behind the other. It was a thing of beauty.

Ann's father, who had never been in an airplane, came out to the base to see us fly. He stood with Ann to watch the show, and afterward she asked, "Well, Daddy, what do you think?"

Not missing a beat, he said, "I think Dick is a damn fool!"

All I know is that flying was in my blood. I loved teaching others to fly as well. I had another unique opportunity while at Lackland. NASA was conducting research that included an eight-day, eight-hour-a-day physical just to enter the program. I was selected to participate in the Space Capsule Testing Program, which was conducted at Brooks Air Force Base, about seven miles southeast of San Antonio. My general granted me time to be involved in the program that consisted of a thirty-day test in a simulated space chamber or capsule.

The physical was very similar to an astronaut's required physical. Some of the criteria for the testing was interesting; we were really guinea pigs in a lot of ways. For one procedure, the technicians put a device on the salivary gland in our mouths, then gave us a piece of gum to chew. From a tiny tube, saliva would go into a small vial, and they thought they could get as much information from that specimen as from your blood. I don't know where that experiment ever went. They examined the heart of each participant for one entire day. One related activity was to put you in a bed in a caged area and take Polaroid pictures of your heartbeat. They did some other stress-type exercises, but to me it was all fascinating.

When the results came back from the medical workup, they then conducted brain wave tests. The results confirmed that I had an abnormal brain wave, probably resulting from six concussions, and would not be able to continue in the space program. It was a variable they did not want to work with. I understood but was very disappointed. The series of concussions, beginning with the accident at the ice company when I was a youngster along with those suffered later on the football field, would have lifelong consequences, one would ultimately affect my great love for flying.

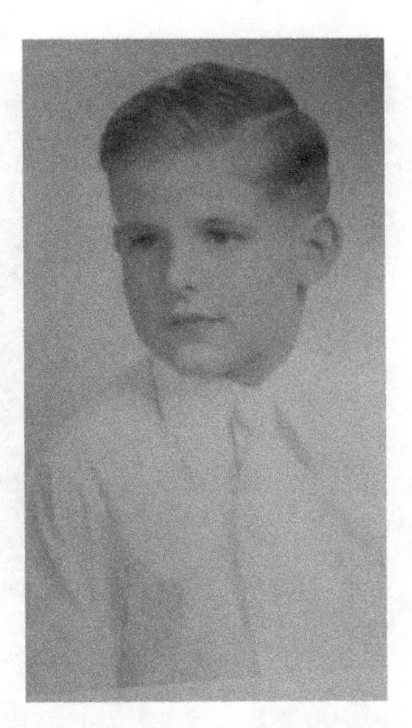

Early photo – think I was around 5-years-old.

St. Ignatius High School Champs 1950 – I'm in the second row, right of center, # 53.

Playing for University of Detroit, 1953 Game.

Escorting Military Ball Queen in 1955 – University of Detroit ROTC.

Finally got my “Yellow Rose of Texas” – Wedding Pic, 1956.

Honeymoon Dinner in Houston, Texas.

Our little Tammy, cheering for the Warhawks
at Lackland Air Force Base.

Our cute second daughter, Teresa Marie, around five years of age.

The Warhawks Demonstration Team 1961.

Coaching at Air Force Academy. Here with Kenny Hamlin who insisted I attend an FCA Meeting.

~ 3 ~

They Called Me "Coach"

In the early 1960s, the results of my brain wave tests, with evidence of prior concussions, was reported to the Air Force. In 1961, they granted me a waiver, giving me permission to continue to fly. Along with flying, I was playing and also coaching our football team at Lackland and having a lot of fun. We played other teams across the country, including the Marines from Quantico, Virginia.

I tried to make time for my family too. I remember when Tammy was only around six weeks old I brought home a little black puppy hidden inside my jacket. Ann, who had always had a dog, was delighted to have Cinder. Tammy grew up around Lackland Air Force Base and became a fixture at all the football games. She was two years old when Ann would bring her to the football games dressed in a cute cheerleader outfit. She would jump up and down on the sidelines and basically charm everyone who met her. She would also go to parades and sit in the reviewing stands.

To help coach the team, I drew upon the experiences I had with coaches as a youngster. Like most everyone who played any kind of organized sport, I had some good coaches and some lousy ones too. I had one coach while at the University of Detroit who seemed perpetually angry. He would get upset and really lose it. I recall he chewed green chlorophyll gum all the time, and he would become so angry that he would literally foam at the mouth with this green stuff spewing out all over. He left, and a great coach came in by the name of Bob Dove. I learned so much about football and life from Coach Dove who had played for the Detroit Lions.

Most men who have played football, whether in high school or on the college level and even in the pros, often say how they miss playing the game even years afterward. The legendary coach of the Green Bay Packers, Vince Lombardi said, "Football is like life—it requires perseverance, self-denial, hard work, sacrifice, dedication, and respect for authority." That about sums it up. But I found other things in life to be significant.

Football is a team sport. It takes everyone performing well to win. Then there's the excitement surrounding the games, the crowd, rivalries, the cheerleaders, the band. And there is *nothing* like standing in the football stadium at a place like Notre Dame as the Irish take the field. I'll never forget my first time there. Your pulse rate quickens, and you feel the whole place rocking underneath your feet from the noise of cheering fans. Football is a game that conjures up intense passions and extreme loyalty. I like what President Eisenhower said, "An atheist is a man who watches a Notre Dame vs. Southern Methodist University game and doesn't care who wins."

I didn't realize I would have another opportunity to coach football a few years down the road. I loved the guys on the team at Lackland and felt honored to be coaching them.

I will tell you straight, however, that I didn't like to lose. Sometimes a loss was a little hard to shake off even though I tried not to take the disappointment home with me. Ann learned early on that even twenty-four hours after a loss was not a time to critique the game or offer an opinion. She was wise to tiptoe around the subject for a few days.

Tammy was two years old when our second daughter, Teresa Marie, was born. She was a very sweet baby even though she had painful ear infections that resulted in high fever. Many times Ann would sleep next to the baby's crib and keep her hand on Teresa as she slept because she was so concerned about the spiking fever. We spent a short time in Montgomery, Alabama, where I completed Squadron Officers School (SOS). While there I we took Teresa to a doctor who advised removing her adenoids. She underwent that operation, and her health immediately improved.

In 1962, I was assigned to Williams Air Force Base in Chandler, Arizona, southeast of Phoenix. I missed coaching the football team at Lackland but was doing what I loved as a flight instructor. At that time, I was training new students in the T-33 and other instructors in flying the new jet trainer, the T-38; the plane was just entering the inventory. I had been programmed to instruct in the F-5, a light combat jet, which had the same basic airframe as the T-38.

One reason I was excited to go to Williams Air Force Base was because Jim Ellis, my right wing man on the Warhawk team, was also an instructor there. Jim was killed in an aircraft accident-a loss to the Air Force and the Abels. This was our first experience dealing with grief.

Then, my life changed dramatically, and I just couldn't understand it at the time. I took a routine physical that showed the same concussion results as the NASA tests. Nothing had changed. However, this time, the Air Force decided to ground me from active flying—effective immediately. It was quite a blow.

I have tried to see it from their perspective. At that time, there was not sufficient data to determine the risk to me or others due to my history of concussions. Although there was never an outward sign of any deficiency, the brain waves themselves signaled an unknown factor. And because the medical personnel didn't know the potential outcome of such a condition, they simply did not want to take any risk; thus, I was grounded. But God was working in my life and this was part of His plan.

My entire identity took a heavy hit because I had joined the Air Force to fly. Now what? I seriously considered leaving the Air Force. I took some time to think about it and even made a trip back home to Cleveland to talk to some good friends about the decision.

I visited one of my college ROTC friends who lived in a big, nice house. He had become a pilot and flew F100 fighter planes then left the Air Force when his commitment was up to take over his dad's business. It surprised me when he told me he envied me, a man in the Air Force.

"Dick, you know, when you're in the Air Force wherever you go, the longer you are in, you can't go to a base without knowing folks. When you travel, you know your family is always taken care of because of your squadron family. As always happens, the hot water tank goes out, the radiator in the car goes out, the kids get sick etc., etc.—and the squadron mates are there to take care of it. I can tell you, it's not like that in the corporate world."

He made a lot of sense, and when I returned, Ann and I sat down and reviewed where we were and what we were doing. We both liked our way of life. Sure, there were challenges at times, but we felt we were serving our country. So in December of 1962, we decided to stay in the Air Force.

I have to be honest, however. It didn't help my spirits much watching others fly when I was not allowed to do so. So I wanted to get away from the flight line where all the flight operations occurred. I discussed the situation with my immediate supervisor and also General Stillman. Then, a short time later, I was assigned to the Air Force Academy in Colorado Springs, Colorado, as an Officer Commanding (AOC) for a cadet squadron and really enjoyed that job. Training cadets and having influence in their lives was challenging and personally rewarding as I served them. My zeal for affecting their lives continued to grow, and I set my course to affect lives daily.

In addition to my training responsibilities, Coach Ben Martin, head coach of the academy's football team, approached me to ask if I would consider being an assistant football coach for the academy's team, the Falcons. I jumped at the chance because of my love for football and coaching. The academy's very first coach had been Buck Shaw, an NFL coach who had had success in the pro ranks, but he was older when he came to the United States Air Force Academy in 1955 and only stayed three years. After a nationwide search to replace him, the academy considered two men as top prospects for the job—one was Ben Martin, who was a Naval Academy graduate, and the other was a coach by the name of Vince Lombardi, whom no one knew much about at that time. Martin got the job.

For four years, I was an assistant coach, which was like frosting on the cake of a great assignment. I loved the Air Force, its academy, and the people who serve as well as their families.

I discovered one of the worst things a coach can do is to think too highly of himself. If a coach ever reaches the point where he thinks it is all about him and not the players, he's lost sight of the goal of coaching. A coach isn't just training young men to play a game; they are training young men to be men of discipline and character all through their lives.

Then, of course, it goes without saying that coaches who abuse players should be booted permanently from the job. However, some things happen to players that you can't foresee or prevent. Those things stay with you. When I was coaching at Lackland, a young man, nineteen-years-old, died one day during practice. He was an overweight kid, a tackle who did not like to run sprints. Because the entire team had to do sprints, I tried to make it fun by having them compete against one another. During the exercise, this young man knelt down at center field, took his helmet off, and looked completely exhausted. I went to him, and when I saw his condition, I said, "Put your bonnet [helmet] on, and get to the gym!"

He said, "Yes, sir," and jogged to the gym door where he collapsed. He was sent to the hospital but later died due to heatstroke. That was a hard day. We usually put up a red flag if the temperature and humidity reached a dangerous level or weather was unsuitable for practice. The red flag was not out that day, and I don't recall that it was overly warm. Of course, we would not have had practice if the red flag was up. And even though the young man most likely died of a congenital condition, we all felt terrible. Some even thought that it marked the end of the football program, the end of our coaching careers. But the commanding general assured the staff, "Those kinds of things happen. You can't worry about it." Fortunately, I never had to deal with anything like that again.

While coaching at the Academy, I really believed athletics was an important part of the life of each cadet. If a young man (or woman) led a disciplined life in order to be successful in sports, it was natural to carry that trust over to life in general, especially in areas of leadership.

We were training young men at the Air Force Academy to understand that leaders have to earn respect. We wanted to shape them to be "inspired influences," a phrase that defines leadership. I thought there was a great balance between academics and athletic endeavors at the academy, with academics clearly the most important. By the way, I have always been proud that the Air Force Academy was the first of the three military academies to allow cadets to major in several disciplines. That set the benchmark for providing specialized degrees.

In January of 1963, I was offered a position as information services officer for the academy. The job marked the beginning of a public affairs career that would continue through the rest of my Air Force years and beyond.

Ann and I welcomed another little girl to our family in April of 1964. Katrina Lorene was born. We called her Trina, and like her two big sisters, she loved military life. By 1965, we had our three beautiful little girls, and life was generally pretty predictable when I received the disturbing news that rocked the Air Force and the entire country. A similar headline appeared in newspapers nationwide: AIR FORCE ACADEMY CADETS INVOLVED IN CHEATING RING!

One of the first press statements released read:

> Air Force Academy officials stated today that they are conducting a formal investigation of possible cheating activities by a group of cadets. The investigation is to determine whether or not examination materials of certain courses have been illegally obtained and used by this group. The academy operates under a cadet honor code. The alleged violations being investigated were brought to light through the operation of this honor system. In order not to compromise the investigation, the academy will not release details until the investigation is complete.

The scandal at the academy broke when a cadet who was resigning reported knowing more than a hundred cadets who were involved in a cheating ring. Overnight the story spread like wildfire, and everyone from the president of the United States to the typical man on the street had an opinion of what should be done to those who had disgraced the academy. Before it was all said and done, 109 cadets were expelled. The breach of honor bothered me personally at a deep level because I loved the cadets involved, many of whom were guys from my squadron or football players—cadets I was close to. I knew something like this could affect the rest of their lives. One thing youngsters don't get is that consequences for one misstep can last a lifetime. I was sorry for the young men because I knew the scandal would follow them forever.

The cheating incident pained me to the core. I came from a civilian school, and my standard of honor and ethics was clearly not the same as the academy's, yet I learned a lot about honor. I talked to each of the young men involved, and let me tell you, it was not an easy way for them to leave the academy.

I gave myself to days and nights of dwelling on how the pattern of cheating developed and how it could have been avoided. I focused on ways to help the cadets who were named in the scandal and tried to repair the institution's reputation. The public looked on and perceived that the Air Force Academy was broken and blasted it for the apparent "breakdown of honor and ethics."

I helped lead a thorough examination following the discovery. We asked serious questions: Are there excessive pressures placed on cadets by the academic system in place? Is the scoring and testing system fair and attainable for most cadets? Do they have adequate time to prepare and study? We wanted to make sure future incidents of cheating didn't occur.

From my standpoint, we had not adequately trained these young men to embrace the academy honor code, hadn't spent enough time stressing the value of the code in their lives. We just assumed because we said, "We have an honor code," that every cadet bought into it. We needed more supervision in the process. I believed then, and now, there was a great need for education and more of an involvement by the officers in instilling a sense of honor and integrity into our cadets.

Academic standards were high at the academy, and if you had a young athlete who practiced two or three hours on the football field, then returned to his room bone-tired with an exam coming up or a paper due the next day, cheating became the easy way out. In any society, there will be individuals who are integrity driven and those who are not. The academy didn't realize until it was too late that a few cadets began to cheat, and then it became a small epidemic because it was so easy to do and had gone undetected for so long.

As the information officer for the academy, I owned up to the media mistakes we made in regard to procedures and information released to the public regarding the scandal. Three mistakes in particular stand out in my memory:

First of all, as all major news networks and media representatives descended on the campus of the academy, an official silence was imposed that kept the details of the scandal from being known. The information staff were "not to answer questions, say anything, or furnish any information." Basically, we closed the door to the public affairs office at the academy. No media personnel could get access to information because they were not allowed to approach with questions. This unwillingness to discuss the details of the scandal led to bigger problems. When the media couldn't verify details or get responses for the public's "need to know" questions or issues, news writers resorted to speculation, half-truths, rumors, and hearsay to complete their stories. Even *The New York Times* commented on the situation at the academy:

> The national interest in this unhappy situation would best be served by ending any further abuse of "classification" and providing full opportunity for all concerned to state their views. The present policy only leads to suspicions that hurt the Air Force, its academy and the nation.

The Denver Post carried a series of articles condemning the secrecy surrounding the investigation and *The Kansas City Star* wrote, "Apparently the Air Force has yet to learn that the best way to deal with an embarrassing situation is to make a clean breast of it."

Another mistake was made when we alienated the local press connections we had worked to secure through the years. The Secretary of the Air Force sent a colonel to the Academy to handle the delicate public relations problems. The Air Force Academy is a national institution, and the scandal was indeed a black eye for the Air Force in general. Washington outsiders coming into the area did not set well with those with whom we had built relationships in the past. They needed to hear from familiar sources they knew and trusted. As I wrote later in a published article titled "Bad News—and How to Survive It," the situation became ridiculous when the press representatives were told they could submit questions in writing (two copies) that would be answered the same day. We had to get Pentagon clearance for all releases. The writers' antagonism were reflected in their columns. The *Colorado Springs Gazette Telegraph* headlined a story NEWSMEN, COFFEE, RUMORS APLENTY—BUT ANSWERS FEW AT AIR ACADEMY.

Lastly, listed in the article written in 1968 were other missteps made throughout the cheating incident. Among them: failure to anticipate the overall impact, release of information to the press on a piecemeal basis, failure to have proper facilities for the media, and failure to provide sufficient background material.

Of course, much of the summer of 1965 was spent trying to review the problems and recover our integrity as an institution. Embracing a positive approach, we made significant changes. We created a community relations branch to reestablish our standing in the local area. Base personnel were encouraged to join local service and civic organizations. News releases were issued regularly, and media representatives were invited to the academy and given access to cadets and staff officers. I insisted on professionalism across the board including answering the phone promptly and courteously. We felt as though we were making progress, but all of it would soon be put to test.

Amazingly, further cheating at the academy came to surface in 1967. The same jolting discovery propelled a second scandal, once more holding the academy under national scrutiny. This one seemed more disturbing because we thought we had put safeguards in place to prevent such a reoccurrence. However, we had learned from previous mistakes and acted accordingly, especially in regard to releasing information to the media.

Following press release spelled out specifics:

> February 24, 1967
>
> The cadet honor committee is investigating honor code violations by members of the cadet wing...violations centered around cadets discussing contents of examinations with others scheduled to take the same exam later the same day.
>
> March 2, 1967
>
> Members of the honor committee completed hearings on investigations of honor code violations...46 cadets have resigned...34 because of cheating...12 because of failure to report direct knowledge of cheating by others.

The entire incident would cover only a period of seven days, and because of our information staff's quick and professional handling of the matter, I felt the reaction from the public was mostly sympathetic.

As a further step toward more transparency, I made the trip to the Pentagon to brief top level Air Force personnel on the second incident. It was agreed that our office of information at the academy would handle all press relations and news releases. Washington would stay informed and furnish any support needed.

We announced a special news conference to reveal the full story of the second cheating incident and informed the media that updated information would be offered often with questions addressed as they arose. All information presented was pertinent, factual, and truthful, and we assured the media reps that we would make ourselves accessible around the clock.

The results of our efforts to inform was noticed and appreciated. The *Gazette Telegraph* wrote of our actions as "an example of honesty rare in these times. All leadership at the academy was made available to news media so the public would know the facts concerning the present cheating incident. No responsible newsman was denied any information and all questions were answered."

It was a trying time, but good relationships were salvaged, and the lessons we learned would prove valuable and applicable to other institutions as well. I was proud of the way we regrouped and set a precedent for future handling of such difficult circumstances.

As for the young men involved in the cheating scandal, many have gone on to excel in civilian fields and careers. One cadet involved was a football player I had coached who went on to play for the Dallas Cowboys for over ten years. Although most of the young men learned from their mistakes and went on to be successful, the stigma remains even fifty years later after the incidents. It should be a lesson to all of us that conduct matters at all times.

In retrospect, the young people involved in the scandals were great kids who did dumb things. In fact, Ann and I refer to this acronym often: D-B-D. It stands for Don't-Be-Dumb; a philosophy to live by. In my opinion, the first cheating scandal was partly the academy's fault, not emphasizing the honor code The second scandal was due to individual young men who succumbed to weakness of character.

Although we had some trying years at the academy, there were wonderful times as well. One encounter while at the academy would change my life eternally.

~ 4 ~

Jesus—The Life Changer

Before speaking about my own salvation experience, it is important to establish that I had a precious wife who prayed for me daily over nine years that I would come to have a personal relationship with Christ. I am eternally grateful that Ann never gave up on me and had complete faith that one day I would realize that Jesus was all I needed and His wonderful gift of salvation would be mine.

Ann ~

I became involved in Bible Study Fellowship (BSF) while we were living at the Air Force Academy. A godly lady by the name of Morena Downing took me under her wing and lovingly mentored me. Morena had been trained by Ms. Audrey Wetherell Johnson to be one of the original twelve teaching leaders of BSF. Ms. Johnson was a former missionary to China when she spoke to a group of woman at a southern California church. The impact was so great, they asked Mrs. Johnson to conduct Bible study sessions for them. She agreed but told the ladies, "I will not spoon-feed you." That is how the scripture and application materials began to be developed. Soon, there would be Bible Study Fellowship meetings going on around the world, and they continue to this day.

For several summers, I accompanied Morena to retreats held in Estes Park, Colorado. Mrs. Johnson would be there to teach and inspire us. These were refreshing times of learning the inner workings of the ministry and growing in my faith and understanding of God's Word.

I also had the wonderful privilege of sitting at the feet of a remarkable Christian—Corrie Ten Boom. For those who may not know, Corrie Ten Boom and her sister, Betsie, had been prisoners at Ravensbrook, the infamous Nazi concentration camp near Berlin, Germany. They were imprisoned along with other members of their family for hiding and assisting Jews during the war. Betsie would die at Ravensbrook, but Corrie survived to tell her remarkable story. I came to know this amazing woman before her book *The Hiding Place* was written and before she was well known. I literally sat at her feet and was taught by the remarkable Corrie Ten Boom.

Another spiritual encounter affected me greatly. When we were a family of four, still living in Arizona, we met a young Episcopalian priest who enlightened me regarding the Rapture (an event prophesied in Scripture, referring to "being caught up" in the clouds to meet "the Lord in the air." It is discussed in I Thessalonians 4:16, and Jesus also spoke of the Rapture in Matthew 24). Remember, I didn't think Dick was a Christian at this time. He was a very good man, but unsaved.

After learning about the Rapture, I went home, got on my knees, and prayed, "Lord, I don't understand all this, but please just let us be in that place where we [our little family] will all go together." Of course I never dreamed that one day our family would be thirty-six strong and growing. You see, it was what I call a retro prayer. God knew exactly how many family members we would have when I prayed it, and I believe He will continue to answer my prayer as our clan continues to grow.

I tried to live a life that would be an example to Dick spiritually. We once attended a funeral of a man we had known. As we left, I told Dick, "At least I know he's with Jesus."

"No one can know that," Dick responded.

I quickly replied, "Well, I hope I predecease you, because you can know I will be in heaven."

Somehow I felt very strongly that Dick's salvation would come through another man or other men. I was praying daily for that encounter to take place even as we took the position at the Air Force Academy.

Our son, Timothy Louis, was born on March 24, 1966. I knew Dick would be so proud to have a son after our three girls. Tim came along, and we were thrilled. We called him our surprised-by-joy baby. When people asked Dick the difference between having girls and boys, he would joke, "Well, for one thing—the plumbing is different!" He would later add, "Boys will shake your hand or slap you on the back, but daughters…they will hug your neck."

Tim was barely a month old when we all attended the final night for a Fellowship of Christian Athletes retreat. The spiritual encounter I had prayed about for so long finally came to fruition in Dick's life.

—

Kenny Hamlin was an athlete I'd recruited to play football for us at the Air Force Academy. He was an offensive tackle from Rome, Georgia. As a senior, Kenny was selected as the outstanding player for the Falcons. He also happened to be a fine young Christian. It was during the 1965 football season when Kenny started asking me to attend a meeting held every Monday night on campus. It was called the Fellowship of Christian Athletes (FCA). I didn't know much about the organization but thought it sounded like a good idea for young men who might be interested in such a group. As for me, I wasn't interested. I was always too busy to go with Kenny and gave him several excuses not to attend. The most predominant excuse was that my Monday nights were usually reserved for watching football film of the previous week's game and studying film of our next opponent. That didn't stop Kenny from asking me over and over though. In fact, he nearly bugged me to death for at least five straight weeks. Finally, I told him I'd go with him once, just to get him off my back.

The group met in a room in the Vandenberg dorm on campus. There were probably sixty to seventy young men in the meeting that evening, and as I walked in and looked around, I immediately recognized half of them as football players. The meeting started with prayer, then there was singing…really bad singing as I recall. The athletes must have believed in the Bible verse, "Make a joyful noise unto the Lord." Then, there was a speaker for the evening. I left the meeting feeling really glad that I had come. I enjoyed it so much that I changed my priorities so that I could attend the next FCA meeting. Future meetings included films, Bible studies, sharing times, and guest musicians.

I don't know if it was the camaraderie of the group that made me want to be a part or the inspiring messages. It may have been the level of enthusiasm I saw as these young men expressed their faith. Whatever it was, I began to attend the FCA meetings regularly throughout the year 1965.

In the spring of 1966, FCA sponsored a weekend retreat at the Black Forest Retreat Center across I-25 from the Academy, and I blocked off the time to make sure I could attend. On the final night, New York Jets wide receiver, Don Maynard, spoke to the group. In 1965, quarterback Joe Namath had joined the Jets, and he and Maynard began to develop the perfect chemistry that would eventually carry them to great success and a Super Bowl win. Maynard is one of only five players to record fifty receptions and more than one thousand receiving yards five times throughout his career. He would be named to the Professional Football Hall of Fame in 1987.

On the final night of the retreat, which Ann and our children attended, the wives and children were invited to join us for the special campfire service that would close the event.

I had attended a Billy Graham Crusade in San Antonio and had heard the message before, how Christ had died for my sins and wanted a personal relationship with me. But that night at the retreat, I heard it differently. As Maynard spoke, the Holy Spirit opened my ears and my heart. When the invitation came to commit my life to Christ, I didn't hesitate. I had been holding our month-old son, Tim, at that time, and instead of passing him off to Ann, I just stood and went forward with him in my arms, holding him like a football. But Tim, your dad never spiked you—I was careful.

Ann ~
That last evening of the FCA retreat, we were all sitting around the campfire, but I had taken the three girls to sit a little higher up and left our baby boy with Dick. The meeting was nearing the close when I heard the speaker begin the invitation. I began to pray, as I had prayed on numerous occasions before. Then when I looked up, there was Dick walking toward the front with Tim in his arms. My heart was in my throat. I thought, *Is this real? Are my prayers about to be answered?* I could hardly contain the tears and the joy.

I prayed the sinner's prayer and meant every word. I didn't hear angels, no visions, no emotional outburst, just felt an overwhelming sense of peace and an assurance that all was now right, good, and balanced. I knew my life would never again be the same. I made a commitment to follow Christ, and to this day, I'm still amazed that He loved me enough to make me a new creation. Like the old beloved hymn, it was His amazing grace that drew me to follow Him for the rest of my life and beyond.

One of my favorite verses is Ephesians 2: 8—9, "For by grace you have been saved through faith, and that not of yourselves; it is the gift of God. Not of works, lest anyone should boast."

Ann and I changed our priorities after my conversion. The Fellowship of Christian Athletes (FCA) became an important part of our lives. From then on, wherever we found ourselves living and working, we would connect with FCA groups, and our children too would grow up attending the camps and meetings, having huddle groups in our home, and learning more about following Christ and being His disciple. "Huddle" is the term FCA chose to describe local groups or chapters. The groups are comprised mostly of individuals who believe in Christ, but all who have a love of athletics are welcome. The vision of FCA is to reach others for Christ. The huddle groups meet for fellowship, spiritual growth, and outreach. The organization would become even more important to us personally in the years to come.

Later, I will detail how attending Pastor Jim Cook's church, the International Baptist Church in Honolulu, helped me very much to grow in my spiritual walk after being saved. Pastor Jim was a servant leader who preached God's Word. My Catholic background laid the foundation, which Jim built on as he helped me in my spiritual journey. I also appreciated the fundamentals that FCA upheld, primarily understanding the "body of Christ" and how faith in Christ makes us all one body, with many parts (Romans 12:4). I would come to realize that sometimes denominations can be divisive, but our churches should be as open as the arms of Christ—He certainly never turned anyone away. We became very active in church, and both felt more committed to our involvement with FCA.

I think back often on that night in Colorado in 1966 when I gave my heart to Christ. Where would I be if Ann had not loved me enough to persistently pray for me? What if I had not been grounded from flying (which was so difficult to take at that time) and assigned to the Air Force Academy? What if a young cadet had not hounded me to go to a meeting—a meeting that would lead to a decision that would determine my eternal destiny? How could I have handled the positions, the pressure, the upcoming roles I would play in a tumultuous world without divine guidance? I have learned that nothing happens to the believer accidentally. I trust Him with His plan for my life. I thank God for grace... His amazing grace. I would need it more than ever in the years to come.

~ 5 ~

Headed to Vietnam and That "Crazy, Asian War"

In 1967, after the cheating scandals were laid to rest, the academy attracted even more attention when we had to deal with the first ever court martial of a cadet. The student was going over the fence at night and robbing convenience stores in the area. He was caught, arrested, and faced a trial. The Academy Public Affairs office applied the lessons learned in response to the scandals and did a very good job controlling the flow of information and dialogue between the academy and the press regarding the trial. We kept the media updated, briefing them on what went on in the courtroom each day. It was a bad-news story, which was reported factually, and that is the best you can do with a bad-news story. It made the front page of the newspapers for three days straight. The outcome? The cadet had a pretty good attorney, and they won the case on an insanity plea.

Our Air Force Academy in Colorado Springs is one of the most beautiful campuses anywhere, and my family loved living in Colorado surrounded by the majestic Rocky Mountains. So when word came in 1968 that I had been selected to go to Southeast Asia as chief of news media for the 7th Air Force, I had some mixed emotions. Serving my country was my job, but leaving my family for a year was a major concern to me. The Vietnam War was in full swing at that time, and we had already seen scores of former cadets deployed to Vietnam, and we knew some would not make it back alive, which pained us deeply. These were *our boys* whom we loved as our own.

The war had roots dating back to 1862 when Vietnam became part of the French empire. Japan had tried to invade the country before Communist China got involved. The French withdrew their military from the country in 1955, and guerilla warfare ensued between South and North Vietnam. The Russians were also helping the north with weaponry and training while American military advisors had been killed there as early as 1959. By 1963, President Kennedy had sent fifteen thousand military advisors to assist South Vietnam.

Following the Gulf of Tonkin Resolution, which allowed the US bombing of North Vietnam, the first American troops arrived in March of 1965. By 1966 there were 400,000 troops stationed in Vietnam. As the American presence there grew to 540,000 troops, the Viet Cong and North Vietnam launched a major initiative called the Tet Offensive on January 30, 1968. South Vietnam and our US military were caught totally off guard. Nearly 4,000 Americans made the ultimate sacrifice during the ensuing attacks. The entire nation seemed shocked at the news, and it brought on major disillusionment due to the optimistic early reports that the war was going well. President Johnson's conduct of the war was widely criticized, and demonstrations against the war, some very violent, were taking place on nearly every US college campus. Protestors, here and abroad, decried our involvement as the death toll continued to mount. This was the atmosphere of the country as I left the Academy to serve in Vietnam, first as chief of news media, then later, as chief of combat news, under General George S. Brown, head of the 7th Air Force. The job would include alerting the media in all aspects of combat news—including interviews of pilots—in order to keep the American public informed and aware of the war efforts.

I prepared to go to Vietnam very soon following the Tet Offensive of January, 1968, but following my decision to make Jesus the Lord of my life, there was another important mission I embraced. With a new perspective on life, I desired to grow in my relationship with Christ and took seriously His directive that all believers should be soul-winners according to Matthew 28:16–20. I prayed that God would give me opportunities to be part of that process. I knew Ann and others were praying for me as I left for Southeast Asia. This knowledge gave me a measure of peace only God can provide, the "peace that passes all understanding."

Ann ~

When Dick received his orders for Vietnam, I began to ask the Lord to place a Christian man in his life while he was there. Because Dick was a fairly new Christian, I wanted him to have the influence of a godly man, a friend he could learn from and with whom he could have fellowship. My prayers were answered when Dick ended up with Don Hilkemeier, affectionately known as Hilky, for a roommate. Don was a mature Christian, and Dick knew from the beginning of their relationship that they would be lifelong friends. He and Dick attended Bible studies together and also went to church on Sundays at the base chapel.

God also provided Dick with a great friend in Steve Taylor who was a naval officer. Dick later would work for Admiral John McCain at Pacific Command, and Steve also was on the admiral's staff. Steve lived a godly, exemplary life, and Dick enjoyed his company. I know for sure that men need other men; they validate one another and become accountable to one another. I would be so grateful that God placed Hilky and Steve in Dick's life.

There was another man, a colonel who was Dick's superior in Vietnam, who was definitely not a good influence. The man was a philanderer and womanizer who often tried to get Dick to join in his carousing. He was married but had a mistress while in Vietnam. Dick told me that the man was a good leader in many ways but certainly not a morally strong man.

While Dick prepared to go to Vietnam, we decided that the children and I should go to my home at San Antonio while he was away. My parents were there, so we rented a house not far from them. I prayed continually for Dick's safe return to us.

Once in Vietnam, I traveled around with members of the media and even flew some combat missions with a squadron commander in A-37s so I could relate the experiences to the media. We also took media on some combat missions so they could have the experience. A fellow coach at the academy was the squadron commander.

I learned quickly after arriving in Vietnam that some media personnel would have their own perspective of the war, and there wasn't much I could do to influence them. A few journalists even had their sights set on winning a Pulitzer Prize, instead of covering the war news in a balanced way. I strongly believe that news, whether it be for print or radio or television, should be reported factually in an objective, nonbiased way. In my opinion, media had a major impact on the attitude of the American public regarding the war. They created a political environment that made it difficult for the leadership in Washington to make tough decisions.

Plus, some members of the media wanted free rein to be anywhere they desired, which was dangerous for everyone, especially noncombatants, while military operations were going on. I was responsible for the media who wanted to be out in the field and on the ground with active units. We had to feed them, fly them around in helicopters, drive them in our vehicles, even provide them with medical care and clothing while there. I've always thought it would be interesting to know how much it cost to support media activities during the Vietnam War. You could call it "The Cost of the Care and Feeding of the Media in Southeast Asia." I would imagine the dollar figure would be very, very high.

I went to Vietnam believing that we were making some progress in the war, but it was very slow. I had the feeling that I didn't have all the information, so I wasn't playing with a full deck. A lot of Air Force guys felt the same, that the United States had the power to go in and clean their (North Vietnam's) clock and take names but couldn't or wouldn't for reasons we didn't understand. We should have done in 1965 what we ended up doing in December of 1972 when Nixon "gave the go ahead" to bomb North Vietnam. Sure, we would have taken some losses, but that would be a small percentage of what we suffered during the total war effort. I'm one that believes that politically, we didn't belly up to the bar and make the tough decisions that would have ended the war much sooner.

I understand how Americans think. Most of us have the mind-set that we always have to wear a white hat, and we try hard not to get that white hat dirty. We don't want to be thought of or perceived by the rest of the world as the bad guys. But it was that kind of indecisiveness in Washington and political waffling that caused our withdrawal from Vietnam to be a long and drawn-out process.

Also, because Russia and Communist China were aiding the North Vietnamese, there was also the threat of nuclear war. North Vietnam was painted by the media to be so powerful that even with our coalition forces, they could wipe us out. The same mentality fueled the same idea years later when some thought Iraq's Saddam Hussein seemed to be unstoppable and capable of using nuclear weapons against us.

I learned during my career in the Air Force and later with the US Olympic Committee that Russians understand strength. (I had to negotiate the wording of a sports agreement with the vice president of the Soviet Olympic Committee). Soviets understand strength and commitment, and when you don't show either of those, strength or commitment, they will run all over you so you don't have the willpower to use the strength you have. That is what happened in Vietnam—we were tentative. I really believe we learned some valuable lessons in Vietnam that we applied later to the war with Iraq.

Let's say we bombed Hanoi in 1965, like we did Baghdad, and knocked out their command, control, and communications. There again, we may have had a high number of casualties, but put it in balance with the final loss of American lives in Vietnam, somewhere around fifty-eight thousand. That number would have been lower, and the negative impact to our country would have been lessened if we had acted faster and with more force.

I was not made aware beforehand of the so-called secret bombing of Cambodia that took place in March of 1969. I knew it had happened, and we started some of the reporting of it later, but I was not cut in on the operation. But those things didn't bother me. When you are in a war, there are things that have to be kept secret if you are to maintain the integrity of the mission. The same is true about countries or factions in negotiations. In my opinion, the status should not be made public. You are talking about a war scenario. Take for example, negotiations on hostages being held in the Middle East. Should that be in the press every day? I say *no*, because our enemies will use anything against us, limiting our ability to negotiate, to wage war, and may even endanger American lives.

I'm proud of our work in Vietnam under General George S. Brown. We made great efforts to provide factual news stories on battle engagements and the outcomes. Every night for a year, part of our team would go down to the Military Assistance Command, Vietnam (MAC-V) press briefings, called the Five O'clock Follies. We weren't the briefers, because the briefers came out of MAC-V, but we were the backup. We tried to get as many crew members down to talk about any significant missions. Things that probably were the greatest challenges were when United States or allied soldiers were killed by friendly fire or when the Air Force inadvertently would drop weapons.

Ann and I had been praying that my remote assignment to Vietnam would not last a full year. Thirty days before my termination date, my dad had emergency surgery, and I was granted compassionate leave to return to the States. Dad made a full recovery, but because I had less than thirty days on my assignment and orders for my follow-up position, I didn't have to return to the combat area.

After those eleven months with the 7th Air Force in Saigon (I was a major at this time), I went to Pacific Command at Camp H. M. Smith in Hawaii to work under Admiral John S. McCain Jr. In October of 1967, the admiral's son, John, a Navy pilot on a bombing mission over Hanoi, had been shot down, was seriously injured, and taken prisoner by North Vietnam. This is the same John McCain who is now the respected United States Senator from Arizona.

Here I was an *Air Force* guy working as the Director of Media on a *Marine* base for a *Navy* Admiral. It would be a great experience. No sooner had I arrived in Hawaii, I was joined by good friend and Navy Commander, Steve Taylor, whom I had met in Vietnam. Steve would be my deputy, also working under the Admiral. And in an ironic twist, the same colonel that Ann had misgivings about, the one who was the Director of Public Affairs in Vietnam also joined us in Hawaii, and was my immediate supervisor.

We continued to work on Vietnam actions since that was part of the Pacific Command. There were hundreds of press conferences scheduled when the Admiral returned from visits to the war zone or when the Secretary of Defense would pass through Hawaii on his visits to Vietnam. In addition, we were assigned to work the presidential visits to Oahu. I cooperated with the White House on visits by President Richard Nixon five times and also handled three visits by Vice President Spiro Agnew over the course of time there, along with many other dignitaries. We hosted many distinguished visitors, both foreign dignitaries and those from the United States.

I received many thank-you letters from several VIPs regarding the presidential visits while at Pacific Command. John McCain Sr., our Pacific Commander in Chief, wrote, commending me:

> For the outstanding manner in which you performed your special duties as the press project officer during the recent visit to Hawaii of the President and his staff. This stopover, a part of the President's trip to the People's Republic of China, demanded and received absolutely faultless handling in the areas of public information.

Our Vice President at the time, Spiro Agnew, sent the following personal note:

> Please know of my appreciation and that of my staff for the great help you have given us during our visits to Hawaii and the Pacific area.

This note was sent to my superiors from Gerald Warren, who was the deputy press secretary for Nixon:

> Major Abel consistently conducted himself in a most professional manner by providing essential services to the White House staff on our various stops in Hawaii. Major Abel is an exemplary officer and does great credit to the Air Force.

Kind words, but it was my honor to serve in that capacity.

I never realized that in my position as an information officer for Pacific Command that I would be responsible for other random tasks I couldn't have foreseen: transporting pandas from China and even an elephant from Cambodia to the United States as acts of goodwill between nations.

In 1971, my commanding officer, Admiral John McCain flew to Phnom Penh on the first ever visit to Cambodia by a senior United States official. Per their custom, gifts were exchanged at the airport upon McCain's departure. For his part, Prime Minister Lon Nol presented McCain with a huge captured Viet Cong elephant. Needless to say there was no room on the plane for the elephant, so we had to go through a process later of not only accepting the elephant but transporting the elephant to a new home at the Los Angeles Zoo. For the Cambodians, giving the elephant as a gift was the highest form of respect.

Working with the State Department, a team of seven was organized to return to Cambodia and oversee the transport of the elephant. The team consisted of two veterinarians from the LA Zoo, an Air Force veterinarian, an Air Force logistician officer, a load master, and I was assigned to accompany the group as a spokesman for the endeavor.

It was in November of 1971 when we rode out to the base camp in Phnom Penh where the elephant was held. Soldiers walked the elephant out for our viewing, and we couldn't help but notice other soldiers looking on curiously as to what we would do with the animal. The vets decided to first try feeding the elephant pellets filled with powerful tranquilizers before trying to sedate him. They placed the pellets in large French bread loaves, but that didn't work. The elephant was smart enough to eat the bread but spit out the pellets. Since elephants love bananas, they put the pellets inside bananas, but with the same result.

On the next day, it was determined to deliver a tranquilizer shot to the elephant. As I looked on, one of the veterinarians took a large syringe and injected the elephant in its rump. I mean it was fast—*bam!* The elephant fell over like it was dead. Suddenly, a host of soldiers raised their rifles and trained them on the doctor thinking he had killed this most prized elephant. You should have seen the veterinarians scurrying around to find the antidote and get that elephant back on its feet.

Sure enough almost immediately after the second shot, the elephant popped right back up like nothing had happened as the soldiers cheered loudly. Whew! Disaster averted.

It was finally decided to load the animal into two revised cargo containers with a large door at one end to walk the elephant in, a door to chain him at his feet, and there was a window adjacent to the elephant's ear through which the doctors could tranquilize the animal while in flight. We certainly didn't want an elephant walking around on the plane while in the air.

We departed for Guam at four o'clock in the morning, then onto Honolulu. From there, one of my staff took over for me and escorted the elephant on to Los Angeles.

The second animal control job I was given was to escort two giant pandas to the United States following the historic trip to China by President Nixon in 1972. During the trip, President Nixon and the First Lady had visited the Beijing zoo, and Chinese Premier Zhou Enlai offered the pandas, while President Nixon made a gift of two musk oxen to China in return.

The two pandas, Ling Ling and Hsing Hsing, arrived in Honolulu to much fanfare. The press was anxious to see the pandas and get the first photos of the pair. They were then flown to the National Zoo in Washington, DC where they lived.

Then, the musk oxen promised by President Nixon came west to go to China, and we followed the same general plan—to make them available to the press for photos.

After these experiences, I felt confident that after retirement I could become a public affairs officer for a zoo somewhere in the world.

Those assignments seem small in comparison to one of the most important projects we worked on while I served at Pacific Command from 1969 to 1972. That was the plan for the return of our US prisoners of war from Vietnam. However, I left the Pacific Command in August of 1972 to return to the Air Force Academy to head up recruiting and the admissions counseling department. One of the concerns the academy had at the time was their attrition rate. It was close to 45 percent when I arrived back on campus. I did a lot of traveling for the academy, working closely with the admissions liaison officers, who were reserve officers serving as our recruiting alumni.

From the beginning, I thought we needed to paint a more factual and realistic picture of cadet life for young men whom we were recruiting to the Air Force Academy. So with a shoestring budget, we produced a short film titled *A Special Kind of Man*. It depicted the early "doolie" days at the Academy through graduation. We filmed cadets in basic training, walking through each phase of training with the premise that it took "a special kind of man" to be an Air Force cadet. We talked about the pressures, the expectations, and even had footage of a "shower formation."

Most outsiders are saying, "That must be where cadets line up and march in to take showers." Wrong. Before cadets hit the showers, they exercise in the hallway vigorously until they are pouring with perspiration. Then, when they really need them, they head for the showers.

Some didn't want to include the shower segment (only about twelve seconds long) in the recruiting film. I said, "Well, you should leave it in the film if we are going to do it. If we're not going to do it, leave it out." The commandant of cadets made the decision to leave the twelve seconds of the shower scene in as part of an ongoing tradition.

We worked and trained the liaison officers to portray the academy in realistic terms. The spiel would go something like this: "Yes, Colorado is a beautiful place. The mountains are great. However, you are going to be in for a real shock. Certain things are going to happen to you. You are going to get your hair cut. You are all going to be in the same uniform. Your only means of travel will be your legs—no cars, not even a bike. You walk or run to get everywhere. There is no leaving campus. Everyone will be treated exactly the same. From that, leaders will emerge..." and so on.

When I left the Academy in 1975 to return to the Pacific Command, attrition at the academy was down to around 38 percent; then, it came down further. That is probably an acceptable number; civilian college attrition is significantly higher. It remains true that some young men (and women, now) are just not cut out for the military environment, the cloistered life, and the demands made on the cadets.

We knew it was just a matter of time until women would be admitted to the Academy. In October of 1975, the President signed the legislation admitting women into our service academies. At the Air Force Academy, we had already thought about uniforms for women cadets and even created the first brochure targeted to women recruits. My opinion? I still believe today, as I did then, that women should have their own service academies. I went to an all-boys high school, so I go back to those roots. We have some storied, successful all-girl schools (universities) in the country. Is there not some validity to having all-boy/all-girl schools? A rhetorical question. Dynamics have changed, and I don't believe it will ever go back to gender separation.

The goal of the United States Air Force Academy, and I'm sure the other service academies, is simply to train leaders. The staff is dedicated to provide the best officers for the Air Force and for our country. In order to do that, young men and women must be motivated. The Air Force provides a great foundation to start a career, to be the best officer you can be. Of course, you can't guarantee that the graduates will make the Air Force a career, but a good job and career opportunity has been provided.

Ann and I, along with family, stayed very active in the Fellowship of Christian Athletes and were involved in good churches. I was growing as a Christian but spiritually hungry for more. I knew God was working out His will for my life, but I could never have imagined being part of the huge historical events soon to come.

~ 6 ~

The Assignment of a Lifetime

Yes, life was rolling along just fine at home and back at the Air Force Academy. I was busy polishing the public's image of our institution and working hard to recruit some exceptional young men when I received a life-changing call. As stated in the previous chapter, when I left Pacific Command in August of 1972, we had been working on plans to return our prisoners of war (POWs) from Vietnam, and I was certainly surprised when I received a call in January of 1973 from the same colonel I knew in Nam, the same one of whom Ann had misgivings. He was now in charge of public affairs and working on the release of the prisoners. The colonel was a good leader but led a questionable lifestyle outside the military. He asked if I could come back and help with the prisoner return, because in his words, "You have the experience of working on the plans."

Peace talks had been going on in Paris between Hanoi and the United States since 1968, but they were often stalled due to North Vietnam's unreasonable conditions. Virtually nothing had been decided as a step toward peace when Lyndon Johnson turned over the presidency to Nixon. Despite Nixon's promise of "peace with honor," the talks would continue for three more years. Henry Kissinger, the Secretary of State, can be credited with setting up secret meetings with a North Vietnamese negotiator outside Paris, aside from the formal talks going on in the city.

Finally, a shaky ceasefire agreement was reached in October of 1972. The plan called for withdrawal of US troops to be followed by a political settlement of South Vietnam's future. One condition Kissinger fought for was the release of all American prisoners of war being held captive by the North Vietnamese.

I had known generally, in broad terms, not specifics, how it would all take place. So when I went to the superintendent of the Air Force Academy in January of 1973, he agreed to release me to go on temporary duty to help with the release of the POWs. My orders were cut for sixty days temporary duty by the Pacific Command. On January 28, 1973, I flew from Colorado to San Francisco, to Hawaii, and then to the Philippines. On the same day I arrived, I was promoted to Lieutenant Colonel.

My temporary duty was to Clark Air Force Base in the Philippines; however, we had no idea when the first release of the prisoners would occur. I arrived on February 1, and almost immediately after announcing that Clark would be the reception point for Operation Homecoming, we set up the press center. Sure enough, media started descending on us. The problem was that we had no information for them, so it was a challenging time. There were probably 400 members of the international press corps just hanging around waiting for any scrap of news.

We tried to keep the media people busy. Visits to the Clark Air Force Base Hospital were arranged, and we made sure they visited the base exchange and took them to the uniform store, the dental clinic, the eye clinic, and the Nightingale Squadron, which was the medical airlift unit. We even took the media people on a minesweeping exercise with the Navy so they could see how that process worked. Some were involved in a Bataan Death March reenactment trip—anything to pacify them, but we were running out of ideas.

Finally, on February 10, we received word that the first POWs would be released on the 12th. There would be three missions to North Vietnam and one to South Vietnam. You could feel the excitement growing on base as news spread that we would finally be bringing our people home. We would be escorting 120 men out on February 12.

I was not supposed to go to Hanoi on the first day. An Army colonel was to be the head escort on the south missions, and the team going north had the Homecoming colonel aboard. A Marine major was also to be on one of the flights and was to escort the third flight from the north.

It just so happened that a family emergency required the Army colonel to return home, so they moved the Marine major to the southern pickup, and I was put on one of the flights out of the North.

There were many details to be covered as we prepared for the missions. For one thing, no free world press were permitted until the final pickup. The press corps were upset because they didn't have access to go north, but we had nothing to do with that. The North Vietnamese were the ones saying *no*.

Included in the preparations for picking up our POWs was the head doctor from Clark Air Force Base. He had arranged for a group of psychiatrists to examine the men when they arrived. The docs offered several recommendations for returning our men. They felt we should take hospital pajamas for them and that a Red Cross tag should be attached to each man's wrist so the doctor on the return flight could do a triage-type report. They also advised that we shouldn't display the American flag on arrival, because, the doctors thought, "It will set the POWs off." They also nixed using the red carpet we had planned on rolling out for the men to walk on. "That too," they said, "will set them off."

I had issues with those specific things the doctors suggested. I said, "You don't know what they are going to be dressed in, and communist press will take pictures of them boarding the plane." I thought it was important they first appear in the same clothing that was given them by the North Vietnamese. And the idea of the Red Cross tag? At that time, all I could think of was a familiar antidrug poster while I was in Vietnam of a dead soldier lying on a gurney with two feet up with a tag that said, "He died of drugs." The Red Cross tag idea was eliminated. As for not having the American flag on site, I was rather insistent on that one. "That's what they've been fighting for. If we don't have a color guard, shame on us."

In the end, it was decided we would not take clothes for the men, we overruled the tag idea, and we would have an American flag displayed. I do appreciate the fact that the psychiatrists thought they were looking out for the prisoners' best interests, but they misunderstood the type of men held prisoner by the North Vietnamese. Most of them were tough, committed fighter pilots, a little different breed than your average guy on the street. We had to do some real arm wrestling with the medical people and psychiatrists but finally came to agreement on the initial handling of the POWs.

A film team was assembled that I had the responsibility of directing. We would take along photographers for still photos and record movies of the events. The media gave each of the escorts a checklist of things (types of information) that they wanted to collect. I remember a few of the items on the list: How did you fly in? What was your route? What was the weather? How long did it take to get there? What time did you land? Who met you when you landed? What did it look like there—the runway, the terminal, the damage done by B52s that hit Hanoi in December, 1972? How did the actual changeover take place? Describe the setting? Who was there? The last item on the checklist as I recall was—any significant quotes?

A communications jeep was aboard the C-130 advanced aircraft that gave us worldwide communications through satellites back to Clark, from Clark to Hawaii, then to Travis Air Force Base in California, from there to Scott Air Force Base in Illinois, ending up at the National Military Command Center in the Pentagon.

The plan was for me to fly in on a C-130 advance air. There would be medical people on board in case they were needed and also maintenance crew for the C-141s on board, because if something happened we wanted to maintain our own aircraft and not have the Vietnamese involved.

I've tried to think about what my emotions were at the moment we lifted off for the pickup. After a weather delay, we got off the ground at 6:20 that morning. The recovery team knew some information and had expectations, but there were many unknowns, and we knew we needed to be flexible. After two and a half hours, our plane was above Da Nang. We orbited for about half an hour, then flew from there up to the mouth of the Red River to Nam Dinh. We were cleared to land and followed the Red River to descend into Hanoi's Gia Lam Airport.

There were thirteen people in the cockpit of the C-130 when we landed. There are not thirteen seats in the front of a C-130, but everyone wanted to see what Hanoi and the Gia Lam Airport looked like, so we all crowded around to get a good view. It was obvious that the airport had been bombed. You could see patch marks in the runway where fresh cement had been poured. Once on the ground, we taxied on the side and were told by the North Vietnamese soldiers to stay by the airplane as exchange negotiations ensued.

It was important to get our communications established and tied in to one of the C-141 planes orbiting above, so one of the first things we did was to unload the jeep and get that process going. I noticed right away that a staging or changeover area had been set up in front of the bombed out airport terminal. Someone in our crew saw the damaged building and remarked, "Air conditioned by Boeing."

We also observed that there were a lot of press present. Cameras with long lenses were taking our pictures from a distance as we waited by the C-130. Mostly, it was Asian, Communist, and Eastern bloc press covering the release because no western press, or free-world press were allowed to be there.

After a couple of hours, the colonel returned with news. "They will release the POWs in shoot-down order with the sick and wounded first, then the eleven longest held. Those are the men who will be on the first airplane."

We were to stay on the flight line side of the changeover area while the prisoners would arrive in buses. Three of the men would be in body casts due to broken backs suffered after their B-52s were shot down. We were told that those men would likely be on stretchers.

Vietnam always felt sticky and hot, like it had just finished raining or was about to begin another downpour. However on that day in February, the heat and humidity barely crossed my mind. My heart sped up in anticipation of meeting the men I'd prepared to receive during the three years I'd spent on staff at Pacific Command. It was quite eerie to look over at the changeover area where the prisoners would come through one by one. The area in front of the terminal was a rectangular shape with wrought iron fencing about three feet high but with openings on all four sides of the rectangle. Tables had been set up inside for the four-party commission members to witness the release. A single table was at one end where each prisoner would come through and stop briefly after their name was called. That was the plan as far as we knew. There was a cover over the table that looked like a parachute. The North Vietnamese soldier calling the names of each prisoner was one who had actually been involved in torturing the POWs.

Suddenly all eyes were drawn to an approaching old bus pulling into the airport. I had a lump in my throat as the bus drew close, then parked to the left of where we were standing. The door opened, and some of the bravest men I have ever met began to step onto the tarmac. They wore light-gray jackets, blue shirts (almost an Air Force blue), with dark-blue pants. I was so glad at that moment that we hadn't put them in hospital garb.

As the soon-to-be former prisoners formed up into two columns, members of the communist press rushed over toward them for close up shots and footage. The men were standing very straight, though not at attention, with eyes focused straight ahead. I quickly turned to our film team and said, "Let's see how close we can get. All they can do is shoot us. Let's see how close we can get anyway."

So we ran over, right into an unforgettable, wonderful sight. To this day, I can't seem to adequately describe the scene. Here were these great Americans; two of them, Alvarez and Shoemaker, had been held captive over eight years. The other nine had been held for seven and a half years. The others were men identified as sick or wounded.

As I walked in front of the line of men in my Air Force uniform and looked into their eyes, I saw the quick winks, the smiles; then, just as quickly, the men would go back to expressionless, placid faces because they realized they were still under enemy control. But I saw the light in their eyes that told me they knew this was real—they were going home. I have never been prouder to be an American or in the armed services as I was on that homecoming day in Hanoi.

Then, suddenly, one POW, a tall Air Force Lieutenant Colonel, stepped out of the line holding up what looked like a white handkerchief with something in Vietnamese written on it. It was quickly snatched out of his hand, and he was pushed back in the line.

"What did that say?" I asked the interpreter near by.

"God bless America," he answered. The officer hadn't been released as yet but had taken the opportunity and the risk to make a final statement after seven years of captivity. It still brings tears to my eyes to think of his courage that day.

Then each man's name was called. As mentioned, I would later discover that the North Vietnamese guard calling out the names was referred to as "The Rabbit," one of the prison camps worst antagonizers. As each man stepped forward, they saluted and were greeted by Colonel Lynn. Saluting in itself was not an easy task for some of the men. US Navy Commander Dale Osborn saluted even though his arm was severely withered and actually had a section cut out of it. You could tell it pained him, but nothing was going to keep him from offering that salute.

John Pitchford, an Air Force lieutenant colonel, came forward to salute, but his right arm had no muscle control and hung limply at his side. So he saluted smartly with his left hand instead. As they passed by, the men said things to me like, "You're beautiful," "God bless you, you look great," "Thanks for coming to get us, you are beautiful to see." I had never been told I was beautiful in my life! Emotions were so high; however, you could tell many of the men were on the verge of breaking, and we had discussed what we wanted to say at that moment. It was to be something positive but not anything that would cause them to break down emotionally or shed tears.

Then, an interesting dynamic took place. Without any prior plan to do so, the C-130 crews spontaneously came forward to escort each POW to the waiting C-141. They would escort one man to the pickup aircraft, then come back for the next returnee. When all were aboard, the C-141 crew chief and I were the last to board.

At first, the forty POWs, including three in body casts, were calmly in their seats because the communist press were still shooting pictures inside the plane through the dropped ramp in the back. They were in very quiet conversations with the crew. I jumped in through the side door, and the ramp went up. As soon as it closed, absolute bedlam broke out!

As the engines started, these men who had experienced extreme torture, deprivation, and humiliation at the hands of our enemies were jumping over the seats, some were crying, some shouted for joy. They were hugging each other, hugging the nurses on board, which made sense to me after all their years in prison. It was glorious pandemonium inside the plane. The plane was taxiing as the celebration continued. As we approached the runway to take off, one of the nurses got on the speaker system and said, "If you don't sit down and strap in, we're not leaving." In two seconds, everyone's butt was in their seats! They were ready to get out of there, which is probably one of the biggest understatements ever.

I realize as I reflect on those moments, there is no way to adequately describe them. It truly was one of those "once in a lifetime" events where you just had to be there to understand. The plane was at the end of the runway, and I was seated next to two of the POWs Larry Guarino and Quincy Collins, both Air Force pilots, as the plane powered at 100 percent, and it shuddered against the brakes. The field was fairly short, and we were pretty well loaded when suddenly the brakes were released. It was as quiet as a church in the back end of the plane where the passengers sat. All talking had ceased.

Those who fly know that at a certain air speed, you rotate the aircraft and hold that takeoff attitude. Then, the struts extend, and the wheels come off the ground. Because all the POWs on board were pilots, they felt it and knew the second those wheels left the ground. Over the noisy power of four engines at 100 percent, I could hear the cheering break out once again as the men shouted, clapped, and waved their arms in celebration. It was true, *they were going home!* That marvelous scene remains locked in my memory forever.

I looked back at the men after the first moments of exultation. A few sat in their seat with reflective stares, almost trancelike. I wondered if they were replaying the seven or eight years they had gone through. Tears began to stream down their cheeks. We were up into the air now, and once again, as soon as the seat belt light went off, they were up again dancing in the aisles and all over the airplane. I thought, *So this is how it feels to be free.*

During the two-and-a-half-hour flight, the former prisoners asked questions with Gatling gun urgency. They grilled us on what was going on in the world, wanting to catch up on what they had missed while in prison. They asked about the South Vietnamese. "Are they holding their own?" The men wanted to know what kind of planes the Air Force was flying. Thanks to the more recent shoot downs, they knew about some of the big events, like landing on the moon, major sporting events, but they wanted details. The *Pacific Stars and Stripes* had produced a special issue that covered the preceding eight years so the men could catch up on all current US happenings.

One of the first things the men were offered was a nutrient drink called Sustical. They seemed mystified that the drink was cold. They hadn't had anything cold to drink while in captivity. One POW said, "You know, I've never smoked, but I'd like an American cigarette." Another wanted to hear the national anthem. Many men on that flight and the subsequent flights said their faith in God and in their country sustained them. They indicated a prime objective of the communists had been to force them to denounce their religious beliefs.

Larry Guarino began to talk to me about his internment. He had been there almost eight years, four years of which was spent in solitary confinement. He said, "We were allowed to have a Christmas service in 1968 during which we started singing 'God Bless America.' Me and all the leaders were put in solitary for at least a year because of that."

Larry began to share details of the treatment he had endured. Solitary confinement was time spent in a six-foot by nine-foot cell with a cement slab for a bed and a grass mat. There were no windows. Various means of torture were used to "get the men to talk," Larry said. One method was to tie their hands tightly behind their backs with a rope through the upper arm, twisting it to pull the shoulders out of their joints. Another tactic was to put a steel bar across the ankles of a POW when he was on a cement bed. A handcuff was placed on one hand with the handcuff also fastened to the ankle bar which painfully pulled the prisoner forward. They would be left in this position for days at a time wallowing in their own body waste.

Larry also talked about what they were fed at the camp. He referred to most of it as "sewer greens." He said, "It was extremely rare to get anything with meat in it. Once in a great while you'd find a chicken foot in the stuff, which was a real prize, because then you could use the claw to pick your teeth." Leading up to the release of the Americans, North Vietnam prison officials had ordered that the prisoners be fed a little better in the last few days so they wouldn't appear so emaciated, but they were all still just skin and bones. Chewing gum, lifesavers, and American cigarettes were quite popular with the men during the flight back to Clark.

The senior officer among the POWs on board was Jeremiah "Jerry" Denton, a Navy captain. Jerry had been shot down in 1965 in his A-6 bomber over North Vietnam. Later, we would learn how Jerry endured an unimaginable regime of torture, isolation, and humiliation at the infamous Hoa Lo Prison, or "Hanoi Hilton," as it was called. In his book, *When Hell Was in Session*, Denton says the North Vietnamese tried to starve a confession of propaganda out of him. When that didn't work, he was taken to the meathook room and beaten; his arms were twisted with ropes until he was close to passing out. The enemy also rolled an iron bar on his legs and jumped up and down on it for hours.

Readers may recall that it was Captain Denton who, while a POW, appeared at a press conference where he was expected to denounce America. Instead he famously blinked the word *torture* in Morse code during the interview. The message was picked up by naval intelligence and was the first indication of what the prisoners were being subjected to. His captors then asked, "What do you think of your government's war?"

Denton replied, "Whatever the position of my government is, I believe in it, yes, sir. I'm a member of that government, and it's my job to support it, and I will as long as I live." That answer cost Denton a torment so horrible that he prayed he wouldn't go insane. He was moved to a prison reserved for those who incited others to defy camp authority, and as Alvin Townly wrote in his book *Defiant*, "Prisoners held there overcame more intense hardship over more years than any other group of servicemen in American history."

This was the man I was speaking to on our flight to Clark Air Force Base. I told Captain Denton the specifics about what would happen when we arrived back on base. We wanted him to be well-versed because media would be there. We knew the only press he had been exposed to while in Hanoi had been for propaganda purposes. It was important that he understood the free-world media would be present.

Jerry listened as I told him we would like for him to make a statement upon arrival. Then the plan was for each man to exit the plane in shoot-down order, and they all knew what that order was. He immediately offered about three sentences that just blew me away. He had really thought through what he would say should the moment come. He said, "Oh, don't be surprised. Remember, we've prepared for this day for a long time."

A few days later, either the *New York Times* or CBS (don't recall which) alleged that we had written the statements for the men, which was absolutely not true. I only wish I could write as well as Captain Denton spoke that day.

Jerry Denton turned to me and said, "I'd like to take the POWs to the back of the plane, where some of them are on stretchers. Don't want any traveling staff, no crew chief, no nurses or doctors, nobody else. I just want to have a meeting with my troops."

"Of course," I said. It was then that I really discovered the impact of the Fourth Allied POW Wing. They had been an operating organization even in prison. The group would change as more senior people would come in, or some would die, but they would adjust to whatever was needed. They, in fact, maintained a discipline within the prison camp, within the POW group. The Fourth Allied POW Wing had already been in place, and I could now see it operating right there before my eyes.

Thirty minutes before landing at Clark Air Force Base, I had gone to the cockpit to send word ahead that Captain Denton would indeed be making the arrival statements on behalf of all the troops and that we would call out the names of each prisoner as they came down the ramp. Each POW would be recognized, then board the bus along with the men on stretchers, and be taken to the base hospital.

As I returned from the cockpit, Larry Guarino, whom I had been speaking with earlier, was at the galley having a cup of coffee. I joined him and felt led to ask, "Larry, how did you make it through those nearly eight years you were gone? Just thinking about some of the things you have already told me in the last two hours just boggles my mind."

Larry, who was about five feet, nine inches tall, looked up at me, and tears came to his eyes. Unwavering, he answered, "Dick, if it wasn't for Jesus Christ, I never would have made it. When I was walking up and down those muddy hills and they were beating me on my back, I could look up and see Jesus, and he looked down at me and said, 'Larry, you'll make it. Remember when I climbed the hill, I had a cross on my back.'"

I've heard many priests, pastors, and preachers talk about a relationship with Christ, but nothing affected me like those words from surviving POW Larry Guarino.

The excitement was palpable as we landed at Clark. It was quite a scene at the base. Crowds had gathered, and the closer we got, we could hear the chants, "Welcome home! Welcome home!" The cheers increased as Captain Denton stepped out. All of it had a tremendously uplifting effect on the men.

Captain Denton stepped forward to make his brief arrival statements. They were simple but powerful words. "We are honored to have had the opportunity to serve our country under difficult circumstances. We are profoundly grateful to our commander in chief and to our nation for this day. God bless America." Then he saluted the colors and made his way to the waiting bus. I called out the returning men's names as each exited the plane, then walked to the bus. The men on stretchers were loaded on, and the busses departed.

Moments later, I started the press briefing using the checklist that the press had given me before the pickup. Toward the end of my remarks, I paused at the request for "significant quotes." I said, "Well, one man said, 'I can hardly wait to get back to Agnes's mushrooms,' and I didn't know what that meant, but it had meaning for him." Then I shared what Larry Guarino had told me of how Christ sustained him through his POW ordeal.

When I finished, I looked over the assembly of free press on the tarmac and noticed Liz Trotta, the tough veteran reporter for NBC. Liz stood there applauding and weeping openly. I saw Keyes Beech, a salty old dog of a war correspondent with the *Chicago Tribune* in the press center, and he said, "I've covered WWII, I covered Korea, and now Vietnam. I've never heard anything like Larry Guarino's statement."

Dr. William Ord was the hospital commander at Clark at that time. I remember turning to him following the debriefing with the media to say, "Bill, I hope you're ready for a big party because those guys who were just put on that bus want to go to the officer's club and party tonight."

Well, Dr. Ord went completely pale, and his mouth dropped. I don't think he was expecting that kind of reaction from the POWs. That was the topic of conversation on the plane, and I don't know if any of them escaped from the hospital hat night and made it to the club, but they sure did want to party!

Later that night, we went up to the hospital to look in on the men. The walls of the hospital were covered with colorful posters made by kids from the US American schools at Clark Air Base and Subic Naval Base. It was easy to tell which posters the boys made and which were created by girls. Flowers and rainbows and bright-colored posters by girls stood in contrast to the boys' posters, which included lots of tanks and airplanes!

For dinner that evening, the returnees were met with a virtual feast. There were steaks and lobster, fresh vegetables and scrumptious desserts, just about anything anyone could want to eat. It was a beautiful array. However most of them headed first to the ice cream machine and actually ate the ice cream while going through the line to get other food. Of course, the dietitian was concerned because these men hadn't eaten heavy foods for many years. Fortunately, no one got sick from eating too much. Blander foods were offered too, but most preferred the traditional American fare.

Watching the POWs eat that night reminded me of the eating habits of young cadets back at the academy. Like them, these men also ate like they were completely hollow inside.

I went to bed that night, having been up about twenty-eight hours, thinking about all the things that had happened in my life. I now was realizing why God didn't have me playing football or actively flying, why Air Force Cadet Kenny Hamlin came into my life when I was coaching, insisting I go to an FCA meeting, and you know, it really reinforced that God truly does have a wonderful plan for our lives. I would forever be grateful for having a small part in seeing that some true American heroes found their way home again.

~ 7 ~

The Taste of Freedom

On the second day of their newly acquired freedom, each POW had a complete head-to-toe physical. I went to the hospital to check on them, and the guys were busy getting teeth fixed or replaced, some needed glasses, all were being fed healthy foods and vitamin supplements and being evaluated for the psychological effects of their imprisonment.

Over the course of the next few weeks, the time the returning men spent at Clark and in the hospital would be shortened. Those on the first flight in would stay nearly five days before returning to US soil. The men themselves gave us feedback and let us know what was most helpful and what wasn't so beneficial or necessary during that time.

While at the hospital, I stood in the door of a Marine Captain's room as he talked about being shot down over a particular part of North Vietnam. He told of how he ended up landing in a small culvert, getting out of his harness and thinking about what all he had learned in survival training. He had his gun and his radio in hand when suddenly he looked up and there was a gun stuck in his face. He could do nothing but surrender.

I tried to imagine being in his place as he was stripped naked except for his boxer shorts. His hands were bound tightly behind his back, and at gunpoint, he was marched a long way until coming to a small village. People of all ages gathered and began yelling, screaming, spitting on him, throwing rocks, punching, grabbing his hair, and making him bow in Asian tradition.

"But this one little old lady went around behind me and placed something in one of my hands. Then she stepped back and made the sign of the cross," he said. "Someone pushed her back into the crowd, and we walked for a long way again. Finally the North Vietnamese soldiers led me into a hooch built on stilts because of the monsoon rains. They loosened my hands before they went out and locked the door. I've never been so depressed in my life, lower than a snake's belly. I hurt from the ejection and landing, and now my feet were in shreds and looked like bloody ribbons because I was made to walk barefoot through the jungle. I was in really bad shape. Then, I remembered the lady who had put something in my hand.

"I brought my hands in front of me but couldn't open them at first. I finally forced the fingers of one hand open and then peeled back the fingers on my other hand. There in the palm of my hand were the crumbs of a cookie the lady had placed in my hand."

He grew pensive before continuing, "That one act of kindness helped me to relate to the Vietnamese people in a different way, because I realized that the Jesus Christ who had died on the cross for me had also died for them too." I wouldn't forget that powerful statement.

One POW I visited with had been a prisoner during World War II and was in the last years of his Air Force career when he was shot down and captured for the second time. I said, "What did you think at that time?"

He said, "I thought, oh no, not again. But it was like God spoke to me and said, 'Hey, we've been through it before. You'll make it again.'"

I stood nearby as the former POWs began to make calls home. The base had a bank of phones set up so the men could dial home directly. It wasn't always good news on the other end of those calls. It was difficult for some to learn that wives or girlfriends had married or remarried, family members had passed away, or families had moved. The Red Cross did a particularly good job in dealing with those kinds of issues with the men.

Admiral McCain had retired by this time, and Admiral Noel Gayler had become the Commander-in-Chief of the Pacific Command, so I did my debriefing and "color" commentating on the mission with Admiral Gayler.

Six days later on February 18, I returned to Hanoi. As a friendly gesture toward Dr. Henry Kissinger who had made a recent visit to Hanoi, the North Vietnamese were ready to release twenty more prisoners. Because it was a smaller group, we flew in with only the C-141, but the changeover area was the same. (For the first trip, I had gone in on a C-130 and returned with the prisoners on a C-141). Each subsequent pick up had its own personality, but none were less emotionally charged.

On this trip was a former cadet at the Academy, Kevin McManus. The last time I had seen Kevin I swore him into the Air Force. When he came through the line on the tarmac side of the changeover area, he gave me a big bear hug and said, "My God, Captain Abel [I was a Captain when Kevin was a cadet], it is good to see you. What are you doing here?"

My response was, "I keep close track of my boys." We had a great visit on the return flight with Kevin and his front-seater, Ed Meckenbier, who also went down in their F-4.

That night, I flew out to return to the Academy and was not scheduled back again until the final POW pickup would take place. In the days that followed, I poured myself into my role as director of recruiting and admissions counseling for the Academy, counting it an honor to have been involved in the release of our POWs. I couldn't help but be somewhat amazed at the turn of events that led up to that involvement. In fact, before Colonel Lynn's call in January to come and help, I had prayed, "Lord, if you want me to go, fine. If not, I'll watch their homecoming on TV and be just as thrilled."

But Ann knew I was burdened for the POWs, because some had been cadets at the academy. Ann prayed that I would have the chance to go to Hanoi and share with the men as they were released. I was anxious to learn what sort of faith life existed among the men and if I could be of help to them on an individual basis. When I got the call to be involved, I was ecstatic. As previously mentioned, I had almost missed the opportunity to actually go to Hanoi but was asked at the last minute to replace the army colonel who was called home on an emergency leave. To me, that was a minor miracle. On that first flight to freedom were forty men—twenty-nine sick or wounded and eleven POWs. God had blessed me with a once-in-a-lifetime experience. Upon their release, I was the first American serviceman they saw, which motivated me to look forward to going back for the other pickup.

I didn't have to wait long. On the March 12, Colonel Lynn called me once again to return to Clark. I was in San Diego on a trip with the superintendent of the Academy at the time I received the call. "We need you back here immediately for a special mission," he said. I flew back that evening to Colorado Springs where Ann met me at the airport with clean clothes. I had tickets cut and boarded the flight to Honolulu by way of San Francisco, then took a military flight to Clark. It was a very long day.

On March 18, the third release of prisoners by the Viet Cong was scheduled. We would be picking up 40 enlisted POWs, mainly enlisted men in the Army or Marine Corps who had been captured in South Vietnam. However, this flight would have one distinct difference. It would also be carrying eight alleged collaborators, men suspected of aiding the enemy. This was why Colonel Lynn had called it a "special mission." It was imperative that the pickup go smoothly and that it attract no negative press that would take attention away from the other

POWs homecoming. There were unknown aspects we tried to cover both operationally and from a public affairs side. We even added a few more staff members on the plane because we had no idea what would happen. It was a very high-tension mission because of the collaborators on board. I never learned of their fate after they returned home.

Everything went according to schedule. We arrived again in the advance aircraft following the same route and the same procedures upon landing in Hanoi. There were no indications of any problems with the pickup or during the flight to Clark.

I have two distinct memories of that flight in particular. One of the POWs on board was Major Floyd Thompson who was a United States Army Green Beret. I witnessed a great moment when Sergeant Lonnie Wright presented Thompson with a new green beret we had brought along to present to the major. I'll never forget it. Thompson took the beret and planted it squarely on his head, then said with a huge smile, "They're never gonna get this off me again."

The other thing I recall about that third flight was that we carried the only POW who was a doctor, Dr. Kushner, an Army doctor. He spoke of his frustration in not being able to use his ability as a physician while being held. "Here I am a doctor, and I see the needs of people all around me, but I can't tend to them, because I am a prisoner." He spoke of how important it had been to stick together and support fellow prisoners as much as possible. "You know, unity above self was our motto."

Doctor Kushner also explained the importance of maintaining a level of stability mentally and emotionally while in captivity. "We tried to stay at a status level. As prisoners, you didn't want to get too high or too optimistic. For example, the guards would sometimes say, 'Hey, you're gonna go home soon,' and the guys would get optimistic, euphoric even, only to fall hard when it wasn't true. We lost some men because of that. So you tried to maintain a position of stability, not up, not down, because you never knew what was happening. You were able to exist better at that level," the doctor said. We learned later that some men had died in Doctor Kushner's arms in the prison camp where he was held.

Upon landing, we followed the same routine as before, calling out the men's names as they exited the plane. There was one marine in particular who had not fared well during his imprisonment and had pretty much lost it mentally. Because he was unstable and could become disoriented, we called his name very soon after the man before him to make it easier for him to follow someone down the ramp and out to the bus quickly without becoming confused and perhaps wandering off. The whole mission couldn't have gone smoother, and I was very proud and grateful.

I boarded another flight on March 19 to escort another group of twenty POWs from Clark through Hawaii to Maxwell Air Force Base in Montgomery, Alabama. On board that flight was Commander John McCain, whose dad, Admiral McCain, I had served under for three years. What a privilege to bring Johnny back to the United States after his imprisonment. It was a special joy to be able to call his mother who lived in Washington, DC, and report that their son was on his way to Jacksonville Naval Air Station. John's mom, Roberta McCain, said, "Well, that is a real answer to our prayers." Who could have foreseen that Commander McCain would one day become a presidential candidate and an esteemed senior United States Senator from Arizona? He had endured five and a half years of extreme physical and mental torture.

I was able to visit with Johnny (McCain) while in flight, and the story of his capture has been well documented. It began October 26, 1967, when his A-4E Skyhawk was shot down over Hanoi. He had fractured both arms and a leg ejecting from the aircraft, then nearly drowned after parachuting into a lake in Hanoi. He was pulled ashore by the North Vietnamese who crushed his shoulder with a blow from a rifle butt, and he was also bayoneted. They carried him to Hanoi's main prison, the "Hanoi Hilton," but his captors refused to treat his injuries, beating him and even rebreaking his limbs to extract information. He was finally given medical care when the North Vietnamese discovered his father was a top ranking admiral. After six weeks in a hospital with limited care, he had lost fifty pounds and was in a chest cast.

McCain found himself in a cell in a different camp with two other Americans who thought he would die any moment. In March of '68, he was placed in solitary confinement for a period of two years. When he was offered an early release by the North Vietnamese due to his father's military status, he remained emphatic that those captured before him should also be released. Afterward, he was subjected to severe torture, which included rope bindings and repeated beatings every two hours while he was suffering from dysentery. His pain became so intense that he attempted suicide, only to be stopped by prison guards.

Even after receiving the best available treatment for his war-time injuries when he returned to the states, John McCain suffered many lifelong consequences from the torture, one of which would be the permanent inability to raise his arms above his head. Whether you agree with his political leanings or not, John McCain is an authentic American hero.

Following the escorting of that group, I returned to the academy for a day and a half, just long enough to pick up some clean clothes and board another flight back out to Clark in order to be on hand for the final POW pickup on March 28.

The ten men to be released on March 28 had been captured and held by the Pathet Lao, the procommunist group siding with the North Vietnamese. Like the Viet Cong and later the Khmer Rouge, they were a splinter organization wanting control of the country, too. There was real arm wrestling about this pickup. First, it was designated that no advance plane was to come into Hanoi. So we arrived and stood by the C-141while the senior people went into the terminal. We had had zero communication; then suddenly, with no announcement, the prisoners started coming out of the terminal toward us. We greeted them and ushered them quickly onto the plane.

Of the ten released to us that day, one was an American Christian missionary, another was a civilian pilot, and one was a Canadian Christian missionary. The rest were military men. The changeover of the Canadian citizen took place in downtown Hanoi through Canadian charge d'affaires from the Manila embassy. The other nine US citizens were released inside the terminal. We didn't see them at all until they walked out in a group toward us, quite different from the routine we had seen in earlier pickups.

In talking to the POWs during that flight to Clark, we learned they had been picked up in Laos by the Vietnamese and taken North. They weren't Pathet Lao detainees at all; they were Vietnamese detainees. But the North Vietnamese played that whole propaganda chip, saying, "Oh, we have to consult with the Laotians. These are Laotian detainees." That was a bunch of baloney!

I sat with Major Ed Leonard, a big, tall Air Force pilot who was a 1960 graduate of the academy. I asked him about his capture, and he was eager to give me the details. "Well, I got shot down in Laos, and after shucking my parachute, I heard the enemy around, so I took off running, but I knew they were getting closer. I outdistanced them and found a tree I could climb that was about thirty to forty feet high. I looked down from where I was perched in the tree and watched the soldiers scurrying around and was feeling pretty secure, thinking I was in good shape. All of a sudden, they set up base camp right beneath my tree!"

"Oh man," I said, "what did you do then?"

"Well, for two days, I sat in that tree and watched them. I couldn't fall asleep because if I slept, I was afraid I'd fall out of the tree. They'd send a patrol out. It would return. They sent others out searching for me, and they would come back in to camp. I was wishing I understood their language because it appeared that finally they were getting ready to break camp, and I thought I would escape. I had my radio with me, and I was planning to call in the rescue forces as soon as I was sure the North Vietnamese soldiers were gone. 'Why, I'll be back on home base in an hour, three hours at most,' I thought.

"Well, one of the soldiers on the ground then started putting up a hammock and used my tree to secure one end of the hammock. He then gets into the hammock and looks up right at me, and there I am sitting up in the tree looking down at him. I knew I'd had it, so I just waved at him and said, 'I'm a coconut.'"

It was great to see that Eddie hadn't lost his sense of humor.

Ernie Brace's story wasn't so funny. Ernie was a CIA guy, and after he was captured, the North Vietnamese buried him in the ground up to his neck and left him there for days. When they finally brought him up, he said his skin had turned black.

The next day was March 29, the day of the final pickup of our POWs from Vietnam. Finally, the free-world press would be allowed to cover the event. We didn't have specific responsibilities regarding the press, so we just continued to focus on the safe delivery of our men. The POWs in the last group of sixty-seven men were in much better shape than those captured earlier in the war. They had only been imprisoned for about three months. They had endured no torture, were allowed to live together in groups, and were fed better. Plus, they knew they were going home soon due to serious talks going on between countries. If such a thing is remotely possible, it was a good time to be a prisoner.

We went into Hanoi again with advanced aircraft, and two planes were scheduled in to transport the POWs, but this time when we arrived, there were about a thousand people on hand at the airport. The same time we arrived, a chartered flight from Laos had brought in twenty-eight members of the US press. They had already toured downtown Hanoi, looking over the area and were even allowed into the Hanoi Hilton.

At the end of the discussions on procedures for the release, we were invited by the North Vietnamese to have lunch in the terminal. As a matter of protocol, we could hardly refuse. There was an assortment of food: chicken, pork, some cold cuts, beef, sliced pickles, potatoes, French bread. They also served a warm beer, which was actually pretty good. Then the meal concluded with espresso coffee. Whew—that was some stout coffee! I had it half full of sugar, and I think it still rusted my pipes.

When we returned to the tarmac to begin receiving the first group of forty men, I was shocked to see the crowd had grown to four or five thousand, and the crush of people was intense. After such smooth, controlled earlier pickups, this one was near bedlam. We had a difficult time keeping a corridor open out to the aircraft.

The second aircraft arrived, and twenty-six men boarded after their names were called. The North Vietnamese waited until the twenty-sixth man entered the aircraft; then, the action stopped. There was only one man left now to take home. Before releasing Navy Lieutenant Al Agnew, who was the POW held for the shortest time, a North Vietnamese official made a lengthy statement in Vietnamese of course, so we didn't know what was said.

When Lieutenant Agnew was released, the crowd began to press in as he saluted General Ogen, the receiving officer. I had never been in a mob situation before, and it was frightening. I said to my staff, "Let's get out of here," but we couldn't move. By just bulldozing my way through some press people, we finally made it to the aircraft.

I was curious as to what this POW group's demeanor would be because they had been held for such a short time. To my surprise, as soon as the ramp of the C-141 was shut, shouts and cheering ensued, with slaps on the back and some in tears, just like the previous flights.

These men were up-to-date on current events and happenings back home, for the most part, so their questions were more about what the procedures would be and how soon they would get to their families in the United States.

I talked to the senior official aboard, Air Force Lieutenant Colonel Lou Bernisconi, and he asked if I had a pen and paper. He wrote out a statement for me that he said was written on the wall of the Hoa Lo Prison (the Hanoi Hilton). It was very significant to him, and he wanted to share it in writing. I clutched the note he had written in my hand and then slipped it into a pocket.

A little later, I made it to the front of the aircraft where Lieutenant Jack Trimble was sitting. He had been a cadet at the academy when we first met. In conversation with Jack, he mentioned the same statement Bernisconi had shared and also wanted to write it out for me. Neither man knew the other had shared it with me. Later I would read what both men had written:

> Freedom has a taste to those who fight and almost die that the protected will never know.

To this day, it remains for me, one of the most poignant, inspirational thoughts about what we should hold dear. There is debate about its original source or author, but the fact that the statement was written on the wall of a despicable place where brave Americans were tortured and died is enough to make it sacred to me. The Hanoi Hilton was demolished in 1990, and only a guardhouse remains as a museum.

The stories of physical and mental torture at the hands of the North Vietnamese began to pour out as the POWs were released. Some former prisoners wrote books about their experiences, while others like Captain Jeremiah (Jerry) Denton told his family of the mistreatment on his first night home and then said he never wanted to speak of it to them again. Jerry, by the way, became a United States senator from Alabama and just recently passed away at the age of eighty-nine. What a legacy of faithfulness and duty he left behind. He is another true American hero.

Below are excerpts from a US news and world report article of April 9, 1973, entitled "Torture...Solitary...Starvation (POWs Tell the Inside Story)." In graphic detail, Jerry and other POWs spoke about the treatment handed out by the Vietnamese enemy:

> **Air Force Col Robinson Risner,** captured September 16, 1965. "The guards would tie your wrists behind you, make your arms pull out of their sockets, bend you until your toes were in your mouth, then leave you in this manner until you acquiesced in whatever they were trying to get you to do. Other times a 50 pound iron bar was fastened to my ankles, then tightened with grips causing the pain to rise slowly from the ankles until every nerve was writhing. I myself have screamed all night."
>
> **Navy Lt. Commander Rodney A. Knutson, captured October 17, 1965:** "I was beaten to the point of near unconsciousness, my nose was broken, both eyes swollen shut, teeth broken out. I was then turned over on my stomach in the stocks while ropes tied my arms together, then beaten across the buttocks with a bamboo club until blood spattered against the wall each time the club fell. I was forced then to sit in an upright position on my wounded backside for six days. I had to walk in an 90 degree bend when they took me in for interrogation because the scab forming on my backside had sealed into my flight suit. I couldn't straighten up."
>
> **Air Force Lt Col. John Dramesi, captured April 2, 1967:** (After his first escape attempt) When I was recaptured 20 hours later, I was beaten until the entire left side of my face and head was bleeding and one eye was swollen shut. Then, they put me in leg stocks and I was forced to sit upright for

two weeks in my own filth. I was tied into joint wrenching positions and my body bolted to heavy iron slabs.

Dramesi and another prisoner, Major Edwin Atterberry, escaped together in May of 1969 but were recaptured after only 18 hours. Dramesi said, "After that, the torture during the next six months was unbelievable." Sadly, Major Atterberry didn't make it home. Eight days after they returned to camp Dramesi was told that Atterberry had died of "an unusual disease." Dramesi added, "Some of the prisoners died of neglect, but in Atterberry's case, I think he was tortured to death."

Navy Captain Wendell B. Rivers, captured September 10, 1965: You can get up at 6 in the morning and fall asleep at 8 at night and walk all day in circles around your room. But you have to reverse directions once in a while so you don't fall down. During one stretch of isolation I was fed nothing but bread and water and would cry like a baby.

Air Force Captain Joseph Milligan, captured on May 20, 1966: I suffered from facial and arm burns after being shot down. The only treatment I was given was a twice weekly swabbing of the burns with hot water. The burns were draining quite badly, they were full of pus, they smelled rotten. One day I noticed some flies flying around my arms. I allowed them to land and lay eggs on my wounds. When the maggots hatched, they ate the dead flesh. After the dead flesh was gone, I went over to the buckets in my cell and urinated over my arms to wash the maggots off, tore up a T-shirt and rewrapped my arms. After that they healed."

Navy Captain Jeremiah Denton, captured July 18, 1965: I once was tortured seven days and six nights in a pitch-black room. They beat me regularly and brutally while I was in large traveling irons with my hands tightly cuffed behind me. It was very cold and I had no blanket, no socks, only sandals and pajamas. After four days I stopped eating

> because it required about 45 minutes for me to find my bucket and get into position to use it. I had to search for it by snaking around the floor and feeling with my head. They can do some interesting things with those cuffs. But that blackness and disorientation—mentally I was at about 5% at the end of that period of torture.

Is it any wonder that these brave men and so many others, heroes all, reacted so emotionally as those C-141s lifted off from that airfield in Hanoi? They were tasting the freedom spoke of on the blood-spattered walls of the infamous Hanoi Hilton. You and I can't understand what freedom meant to them because we have never lost it. Operation Homecoming remains for me a high watermark in my entire life and career. What a privilege, a blessing beyond measure to have been chosen to witness such significant events in the history of our country. I often remember some new or additional detail about those days, but I will never forget the unbridled joy demonstrated by men on their way home after enduring the worst things human beings can do to other human beings. Those men and their families deserved every medal, every honor, every blessing our country could bestow.

~ 8 ~

A Look Back at the Vietnam War

After the POW pickups and returning to the academy, I was contacted regularly by various groups and media to recount my experiences related to the release and return of the American prisoners of war. I would deliver over one hundred speeches over the next few years and was honored to do it. It was difficult to get through recounting the experience without tears.

I have spent much time thinking about those men who survived the most atrocious treatment as prisoners of war; some with whom I kept in contact: Ev Alvarez, the longest held POW, Red McDaniel, Paul Kari, and Ben Pollard. I was also in contact with Larry Guarino and Jerry Denton; they have both since passed away. I'm on the mailing list for the NAM POW Group, not that I could ever identify with them, but since I escorted 180 of the 580 returning POWs, I've tried to stay involved with the guys.

I have not looked at the facts recently, but I know five years after their return, the divorce rate among the POWs was about 46 percent, which is now close to the national average for marriages failing. Some of the men just didn't realize that in their absence, their wives had become provider, caretaker, both mom and dad to their children, and took care of everything else. Then suddenly the service member comes home thinking things will be the same as when he left for duty. I don't think either side really recognized the true impact of those long separations. Sadly, I've heard of a couple of suicides among the group. However, for the most part, the men came back and carried right on and some POWs had great personal success after their return.

I know I've mentioned my views on some components of the Vietnam war, but here's something else. I don't think we prepared the Vietnamese military to hold their own after we pulled out, actions we have repeated recently regarding our departure from Iraq. I was discouraged that so many American lives had been sacrificed to see the war end the way it did, without a clear victory.

I've been asked my opinion as to whether there are MIAs/POWs left in Southeast Asia. I think the question has to be phrased this way: Are there any people who are being detained? In 1976, a Japanese army enlisted soldier came out of the hills of Guam not knowing World War II was over. The jungles of Vietnam are so dense and remote it would be possible for one to live and subsist there indefinitely. War in some fashion has continued, and there has been on-going fighting since we left with reports of airplanes flying, as well as North Vietnamese troop movement. I suppose someone on the ground, out of contact with anyone, could still be living in the jungle or caves, unaware of our departure. Or a soldier could have made a conscious decision to blend in to the Vietnamese culture, find a wife, and stay of his own volition. The other possibility is that there are a few detainees still being held.

Just before retiring, Lieutenant General Gene F. Tighe Jr. said, "We may still have some Americans up there." Gene was head of intelligence at Pacific Command and was director of Defense Intelligence Agency (DIA) at the same time. He's a good friend whom I talked to regularly about this. "We have checked out every suspected sighting, and none of them have had validity," Gene told me.

I've read a good portion of the book *Kiss the Boys Goodbye: How the United States Betrayed its Own POWs in Vietnam* by the

Stevenson couple who believe there are remaining prisoners and those who are missing in action (MIAs) in Vietnam. I've talked to retired Navy Captain "Red" McDaniel who is a colleague of General Tighe and even personally asked Senator John McCain about the subject. Red says, "Yes, there may be others." McCain says, "No."

Here is what is known. They (the Vietnamese) still hold the remains of 1,500 or more men—MIAs. For what? Why hold the remains? It has to be nothing more than political gain or leverage. They have released remains periodically, and I just don't understand it. Is their mind-set, "We want something from the United States, so we'll release eight or so sets of remains?" Why do that? Why not just make it clear, "Here is our warehouse full of remains. Take them all. We want to end this whole thing."

In 1975 when we pulled out of Vietnam, again, I don't think we prepared the Vietnamese, although we tried. I think maybe a different technique in that regard might have worked better, but that's 20/20 hindsight. I believe the war could have ended with a more positive position for our country, but that would mean making different decisions during the early days of the war.

The Vietnam Memorial Wall in our nation's capitol is a solemn reminder of the human sacrifice our country made to free a nation from the oppression of communism. Our exit strategy was flawed and probably lacking in courage to do the right thing—prepare for peace. Still, I am extremely proud of the veterans of the Vietnam war who obeyed their nation's call to duty and fought bravely, many paying the ultimate sacrifice to serve our country.

~ 9 ~

Aloha Days

When I returned to the Air Force Academy in 1973 following the POW missions, I jumped right back in and felt like we were accomplishing much in the area of recruiting and admissions. Then, in 1975, Admiral Noel Gayler of the Pacific Command insisted I return to Hawaii as Director of Public Affairs. I was a fairly young lieutenant colonel, and the position is a senior colonel position. Colonels were directors of public affairs or information at the services for US forces in Korea and Japan and at *Pacific Stars and Stripes*, the official newspaper for American forces in the Pacific theater.

Because I was a lieutenant colonel and the position was for a *senior* colonel, Admiral Gayler had to defend me as his choice to some of the other colonels, but in the end made it clear, "I want you. I know what you did in Operation Homecoming, and you are the guy."

I even tried to talk him out of offering me the position, but he repeated, "No, you are the guy!"

So I accepted the position as Director of Public Affairs and was challenged to lead the senior colonels, if you will, for the services and *Pacific Stars and Stripes.* However, I was promoted to full colonel soon after arriving at PACOM Headquarters.

Somebody asked me, "How could you have two assignments to the Air Force Academy in Colorado and the other to Hawaii [two of the most beautiful places in the world]?"

Good question. My answer? "Because the good Lord is my personnel officer."

I would actually have preferred to serve in Europe over Hawaii because I had never had duty in Europe, and both Ann and I are of German ancestry. I truly took the position in Hawaii because it was a challenging job, not just because it is a beautiful place to live.

The family once more settled in and quickly adjusted back to life in Hawaii. We had started Fellowship of Christian Athletes (FCA) Huddle groups wherever we lived, and Hawaii was no different. Ann also started the first Huddle group for girls in Hawaii—called the Cuddle. FCA still has girls' groups, but they do a lot of meetings combined with the boys. In Hawaii, we met as a combined group (boys and girls) once every month and did a good job of planning activities a semester ahead with the help of student leadership. Our own kids grew up with FCA, attending meetings, Huddle groups, conferences, and summer camps.

In August of 1976, other than dealing with the "boat people" attempting to go back into Vietnam from Guam, our first real crisis arose. It is referred to as the "Korean tree cutting murders," or the "ax murders." For those who may not recall, the incident arose in a demilitarized zone between North and South Korea because a poplar tree about one hundred feet in height blocked the line of sight between a United Nations Command (UNC) checkpoint and an observation post. So on August 18, a small group of nineteen soldiers from both the United States and South Korea loaded a truck with axes to be used to trim the tree, then drove into the area as previously scheduled and approved. The two American captains accompanying the group were not armed.

North Korean soldiers showed up and demanded the detail to stop the cutting of the tree. When the United States and South

Korean personnel ignored them, a furious North Korean, Senior Lieutenant Pak Chul, ordered his men to attack. His actual order was, "Kill the bastards!"

The North Koreans grabbed the axes dropped by fleeing tree trimmers and attacked the two US soldiers, Captain Bonifas and Lieutenant Barrett, and wounded every United Nations guard but one.

Captain Bonifas was beaten to death while Lieutenant Barrett jumped a low wall into a low-lying ravine covered with grass, trying to escape the attack. He would later also be found dead as a result of the brutal attack.

Of course, North Korea released their own version of the attack, but they didn't realize it was being filmed on both a black and white camera as well as with a 35 mm telephoto lens. This was their version:

> Around 10:45 a.m. today, the American imperialist aggressors sent in 14 hoodlums with axes into the Joint Security Area to cut the trees on their own accord, although such a work should be mutually consented beforehand. Four persons from our side went to the spot to warn them not to continue the work without our consent. Against our persuasion, they attacked our guards en masse and committed a serious provocative act of beating our men, wielding murderous weapons and depending on the fact that they outnumbered us. Our guards could not but resort to self-defense measures under the circumstances of this reckless provocation.

The CIA stated the attack had been preplanned by the North Koreans, and retaliation actions were discussed. Readiness levels for American forces in South Korea were increased to DEFCON 3 (Defense Condition, Level 3) early on August 19. Rocket and artillery attacks in the area were considered. Back at Pacific Command, we were on alert and got together with the commander of US forces in Korea and coordinated with Washington as to how to mass the forces and go in and take action if called upon.

It was decided that a show of force was necessary, but one that wouldn't cause further escalation. So three days after the ax attacks, the United States sent a clear message to North Korea. On August 21 at 7:00 a.m., Operation Paul Bunyan was underway. This time the tree was not to be trimmed; it would be cut down. A total of 23 vehicles drove into the area without warning the North Koreans. Two eight-man teams of military engineers equipped with chain saws showed up accompanied by two security platoons armed with pistols and axe handles. South Korean special forces were sixty-four men strong on site. They had M16s and grenade launchers. Twenty utility helicopters circled ahead of seven Cobra attack helicopters. Behind the choppers were US F-4 Phantom IIs and B-52 Stratofortresses along with South Korean F-5 Freedom Fighters. The *Midway* was moved just offshore. If that wasn't enough, 12,000 additional troops were ordered to Korea, including 1,800 Marines from Okinawa. Nuclear-capable strategic bombers circled above the scene too. Pacific Command was on battle alert also.

Never before has one tree garnered so much attention and potential danger. When the 150-member North Korean troops armed with machines guns and assault rifles arrived in buses, they had to be overwhelmed by the show of US power. They finally disembarked and sat up machine gun positions but just watched in silence as the tree in question was felled in forty-two minutes. The stump of the tree was deliberately left standing. It was an incident that could have resulted in full-scale war. Thankfully, all was calm after a few tense days.

I was made aware of another incident around two o-clock one morning when a reporter with UPI called me. "I just heard there has been a release of prisoners from China. Are they coming through Hawaii?" she asked.

That woke me up. I said, "I have absolutely no idea what you're talking about, but I'll get back to you." Then, I dressed quickly and made my way to the command center at Pacific Command Headquarters.

Sure enough, the Chinese had released some prisoners through Hong Kong. They were civilian prisoners, Americans, eight in all, who had been picked up as spies in China. They had boarded a C-141 and indeed were coming through Hawaii.

I called the assistant secretary of defense for public affairs. "We have these people coming through here. How do you want me to handle it?"

"We can't tell you. Call the State Department," they suggested. So I called the special State Department contact and told them what was happening. Their only guidance was, "You can tell the press they're coming through. But the press cannot talk to them unless they want to talk to the press." So we were basically playing it by ear.

Eight or ten members of the press showed up at Hickam's Air Terminal just as I arrived. When the plane landed, I walked briskly over to let the crew know what I was doing. The first guy off was Dr. Leonard Jackson, a flight surgeon who was a long-time friend.

"Dick," he said while shaking my hand, "what are you doing here?" I explained my position, then boarded the plane to talk to the senior officer in the group.

"I passed along the word from the State Department. "They said it's up to you individually. If any of you want to talk to the press, you may."

"No, we don't want to talk to the press," was the unified response.

We were interrupted when I was called off the plane to take a call from someone in Washington. The man on the other end immediately began to chew me up one side and down the other. I couldn't even talk because he was talking so loud and fast. Finally, when he took a breath, I interjected, "Well, Colonel, I talked directly to the State Department and followed their directions. That was my guidance, and that is what I am doing."

"Oh, okay," was all he said and then abruptly hung up.

I don't have a clue who he was, but my guess is that he may have been a CIA operative. Afterward, I walked over and held a one-man press conference to answer questions of the few press present.

"Well, how do they look? When can we talk to the commander?" they asked.

I said, "They look well. They are eating well. I talked to the flight surgeon on the flight who said they were sleeping a lot and doing well. As to the commander, he doesn't want to talk to anyone."

A group boarded the plane whom I assumed to be in charge of debriefing the prisoners, and then the plane lifted off, headed for Washington.

We also dealt jointly on the issue of withdrawing troops from Korea. I was particularly involved because of my position, but I think Pacific Command got involved more in the Mutual Defense Board meetings with the Philippines, Japan, Korea, and the Southeast Asia Treaty Organization meetings.

The Pacific Commander, as a senior military leader, represents the security interests of the United States in those meetings. My role, which was very interesting, in traveling with him was to handle the communiqués and the documentation, to be a delegate at some of the meetings and try to manage the press. I saw personally and understood the force structures needed to take place in varied situations, like the Okinawa US Military bases and Clark Air Base and Subic Bay Naval Base in the Philippines. The Pacific Command also had responsibilities in Australia and New Zealand through ANUS (Australia, New Zealand, and United States) treaty. It was all very important work.

Another interesting incident from media perspective occurred in the late 1970 when Major General John K. Singlaub was quoted as going against then President Carter's conviction to withdraw troops from Korea. His statements led to his forced retirement.

Later, General Singlaub was speaking at a college in the southeast and made other negative statements but said he didn't know the press were present, yet there was a visible television camera on site. How can you say you didn't know unless you have an agenda to push personally? Anyway, I dislike those situations that embarrass our country or military. Even with a little public relations or media training, you can answer questions in a press conference without shooting your toes off. This is why Air Force media training for service leaders is so important.

For me, I chose to recognize the authority over me in all situations, and although my personal opinion may have differed, I carried out the message and the wishes of my superiors. If I had come to the point where I could no longer have done that, I would have resigned.

A well-trained media or information manager can get a point across in a circumspect way that can't be taken out of context. It is like responding to questions that begin with the word "if." "If such-and-such happened, what would you do?" Well, first of all, a seasoned professional information officer will not get caught in the speculation business. One can't and shouldn't speculate about events or situations. Don't answer the "if" questions. Each case has to stand on its own merit. In order to speculate as to what should happen "if" something else happened, would be like trusting in a crystal ball, and I don't believe in crystal balls.

Our time in Hawaii was grand, and I traveled extensively. There were forty-four countries within the AOR (Areas of Responsibility) of the Pacific Command. This was a unique time for our entire family. It was during this period, on our first tour in Hawaii, that we sat under the ministry of Jim Cook, who pastored the International Baptist Church. He and his wife Shirley would become lifelong friends. I grew more spiritually under Jim's teaching than in any other period of my life. He took a special interest in me, and I appreciated the way he mentored me with both love and accountability.

We transitioned from Admiral Gayler to Admiral Wiesner during my time in Hawaii. Imagine it. There I was, an Air Force officer, working on a marine base, under my third admiral; however, I wouldn't trade those days in Hawaii. I learned a tremendous amount, and the experiences there were valuable as they prepared me even more for the days to come. I think back on my few short years in Hawaii at Pacific Command and feel confident that God was "directing my steps" and preparing me for the next chapter—my loose translation of Proverbs 3:5–6: "If God directs your steps, don't try to understand all that happens along the way." Below is Ann's account of a particular Sunday while in Hawaii, one that could have had extremely serious consequences, but God wasn't quite through with me yet.

Super Bowl Sunday 1976

Ann ~

Yes, our family loved our time in Hawaii, and we made some great memories, but January 29, 1976, which happened to be Super Bowl Sunday, is a day that would particularly stand out as an unexpected experience. On that eventful day in January, everyone was excited about the upcoming game featuring the Dallas Cowboys against the Pittsburgh Steelers. Even in Hawaii, professional football is taken very seriously, perhaps because it helped those of us living in Hawaii feel more connected to our mainland roots. To make the day even more special, we were hosting a couple vacationing in Oahu whom we knew from Dick's coaching days at the Air Force Academy. Of course, we had a lot of catching up to do. Plans were made to pick them up from their hotel, and they would be attending church with us before coming to our home for our Super Bowl Party. Other friends were also invited to join us in watching the game.

That Sunday morning, I rose earlier than Dick to get a head start on the food preparations for the gathering that afternoon. I am seldom out of bed before Dick, so I thought it a bit strange when I didn't hear him up and stirring. I left the kitchen to check on Dick and found him in the bedroom sitting on the edge of our bed holding his head in his hands.

"Dick, are you all right?" He didn't answer right away, but he didn't have to. I knew something was very wrong. One of his eyes was looking at me, but the other was fixed in the opposite direction. And when he tried to speak, I knew by his slurred words something was happening to him. The thought came to me that perhaps he was having a stroke, but he was only forty-two years old and in great shape. He worked out daily with Marines at Camp Smith, where he was assigned. But when I saw how he was struggling to stand, I went to the phone and called a friend who attended our church and was an Air Force doctor.

"Ann, take him to Tripler General Hospital immediately!" Tripler is a large army hospital serving all branches of the military.

"Dick, we need to take you to the hospital right away," I said, explaining to him what the doctor had told me.

He answered in a strong but still halting voice, "No, we are going to pick up our friends, take them to church first. Then, I'll go to Tripler!"

So I got the children up, fed and dressed them, and off we went toward Waikiki to pick up our visiting friends. When we arrived at the hotel, our friends were waiting for us, but Dick couldn't get out of the car to greet them. As they entered the car, Dick tried to say a few words, and I explained to them, "Sorry, Dick is having a few problems this morning." As we drove to church, I tried to carry the conversation so Dick wouldn't have to try to talk.

Our doctor friend was waiting for us in the church parking lot when we arrived and quickly assessed Dick's condition. He insisted on getting him to the hospital immediately. I had also called a young couple from the church, Dougg and LeAnn Custer, who were like family to us and asked them to host our friends, take them and our children to church, and then to our house for the game...without us!

I was praying for Dick as the doctor drove ahead of us with lights flashing all the way to the emergency entrance of the hospital. Dick was placed into a wheelchair and rushed into the ER as I parked the car. Already he was being triaged by a medical team when I entered the room. Doctors and nurses were working on him. One of the technicians was having a difficult time finding a vein in Dick's arms, and it was obvious this was causing discomfort because Dick sat up and said, "If you don't get that needle in the next time, you're going to be wind up part of the wall!" The next attempt worked. I believe that pain stimulus brought Dick out of the shock he was experiencing.

After tests were performed, the evaluation by the head doctor was sobering. "Dick is having a stroke due to bleeding in his brain stem. If it can't be stopped, he is in danger of either dying or suffering serious brain damage."

As I processed that news, I felt a hand on my shoulder. I looked up to see our pastor who had heard about what was happening and actually left his pulpit to join us. We will always remember and be grateful for our dear friend, Pastor Jim Cook, and his comforting presence.

Word spread of Dick's condition, and many concerned people began coming to the hospital, so many in fact, a hospitality suite was opened to accommodate the crowd. I stayed by Dick's bedside around the clock, leaving only to give periodic reports to our children and friends and to check the Super Bowl score for Dick. Throughout the ordeal, I felt God's peace and presence and knew He was in complete control and would do what was best for us. Finally Dick's condition was stabilized, and he was moved from intensive care to a private room. He was still experiencing eye problems, mainly with focusing and double vision.

The next day, Pastor Cook asked if he could bring some men over who were leaders in the church in order to anoint Dick with oil and pray for his healing. Of course, I agreed. When they arrived, I was cordially asked to leave the room. Some tense moments passed; then, Pastor Cook opened the door and asked me to come in. "Ann, look at Dick's eyes," he said.

I immediately noted that Dick's eyes were focused and alert. The usual sparkle wasn't there, and the clear blue color of his eyes was dulled somewhat, but he was no longer seeing double, and both eyes were in sync! We all praised our Lord for His healing power.

A few days later, I overheard a group of doctors discussing Dick's case. The general agreement was that there was nothing more they could do for him. I interrupted their conversation to ask, "Is there a doctor, a specialist, anywhere in the world who could possibly offer help or have some answers for us?"

There was a long silence; then, one doctor said, "There is a doctor who might be able to help. He is Dr. William Hoyt at Moffett General Hospital in San Francisco."

In short order, the Air Force had arranged for Dick to be medevaced to San Francisco, with me accompanying him as his medical attendant.

We found a room just a block away from the hospital. Soon after arriving, we walked over to locate the doctor's office to make sure where to go for the appointment on the following day. Most of the offices were closed for the evening, but we located Dr. Hoyt's office and found a light was still on inside. We knocked, and sure enough, the doctor himself answered the door and greeted us warmly. We had a lovely conversation about why we were there. When we saw him the next day for Dick's scheduled appointment, it felt like we were seeing an old friend.

The results of the many tests given to Dick were disappointing. After several days of this testing, Dr. Hoyt called us into his office for the prognosis. "I'm sorry, there is really nothing else we can do. Dick, you have a rare malady called stroking out syndrome, and you will probably have more strokes in the future, each one causing more damage." I recall the tears in his eyes as Dr. Hoyt delivered these words, "This is the hardest part of my job."

I have difficulty explaining the peace Dick and I felt after hearing Dr. Hoyt's discouraging report. When we stepped out of the hospital, I recall that the sun was brightly shining, and it matched our emotions. We stopped at the corner and were amazingly elated. "Dick, why am I feeling happy—like it is all going to be okay?"

He said, "Ann, this is the first time that we've had to completely rely on our God…not anyone or anything else." It was truly an exhilarating experience.

Life went on. Dick returned to his Air Force duties without any long-term disabilities from his stroke, with the exception of needing glasses. We rejoiced in God's blessing of healing and did not give in to the fear of reoccurring strokes, knowing our loving God was in complete control.

By the way, the Steelers beat the Cowboys in the Super Bowl of 1976!

Greeting POWs at the first pick-up in Hanoi, Feb. '73 – Experience of a Lifetime.

Escorting U. S. Navy Lt. Agnew, the shortest held POW in Viet Nam to the waiting plane.

Delivering a Press Brief following the first release of U.S. POWs from North Vietnam.

We hosted many celebrities coming through Honolulu here with Bob Hope.

Ann and I hosted Barry Goldwater and wife. Also in photo is Larry Guarino, a POW on the first flight out of Hanoi.

And here is the famous elephant I wrote of; a gift from Premier of Cambodia destined for the U.S. Also in picture is Admiral John McCain, Sr. - father to Senator McCain of Arizona.

FCA Huddle group from Radford High School in Honolulu with visiting Dallas Cowboy's Bob Lilly. God did amazing things in the lives of these young men.

Proud to serve as escort for our third daughter, Katrina (Trina), who was named high school Homecoming Queen, Fall of 1981.

~ 10 ~

Pentagon Calling

Jimmy Carter became the country's thirty-ninth president in 1976 after Nixon resigned amid the Watergate scandal. Gerald Ford finished out Nixon's term. Carter promised, and voters hoped, for a fresh perspective from a leader who was not a Washington insider but a Sunday school teacher who managed his family's peanut farms from Plains, Georgia.

As Carter's term began, there were already rumblings of a crisis brewing in Iran. The Shah of Iran, whom the United States had supported, would eventually flee the country in exile, and the new religious leader, Ayatollah Khomeini, came to power.

Around that same time in 1978, God had another surprise for me and the family, one I wouldn't have imagined possible. General George S. Brown had been Chief of Staff for the United States Air Force since his appointment by President Nixon in 1973. He became chairman of the Joint Chiefs of Staff in 1974. A rather outspoken leader, General Brown got into some hot water over some comments he made. He had also done away with the public affairs advisor, saying, "Let the Department of Defense support me." He would retire for health reasons in June of 1978, and sadly by the end of the year, General Brown died from prostate cancer.

When General David Jones replaced him, Tom Ross, the Assistant Secretary of Defense for Public Affairs suggested to General Jones that he have a public affairs assistant. General Jones agreed and said, "See who we have for the position."

It so happened that I had worked with the Army Chief of Public Affairs in the Pacific, Army General Bob Sullivan. Bob went to General Jones and said, "There is one guy that can do it and work with all services, and that man is Dick Abel."

General Jones selected me for the position of Special Assistant for Public Affairs, without even interviewing me.

Ann ~

The total six years we spent in Hawaii had been wonderful! Our family loved the beaches, the climate, and relaxed lifestyle. None of us were ready to once again leave our beloved island home. We especially were not eager to move to Washington, DC! All we had heard were negative reports until one day I went over to meet a new neighbor moving in behind us while we were living on Hickam Air Force Base. As we visited, I discovered the new family was coming from DC.

When I told her we were soon leaving for the Pentagon, the wife lit up and said, "Oh, you are going to just love it there! We didn't want to leave!"

Her enthusiastic statement changed my total attitude, and I learned that what you expect is what you usually get! So our family began looking forward to this next adventure in our journey with Dick Abel.

The one thing that we would miss the most from our *paradise* experience was our church, International Baptist. We had all grown spiritually while there. We had been baptized in the Pacific Ocean and had made great friends including the pastor and his wife, Jim and Shirley Cook. We'll all cherish the memories of the years we spent there and the strong foundation of faith imparted to us that we've built on through the ensuing years.

When we arrived in Washington in the summer of 1978, Tammy, our oldest daughter, had married Lieutenant Ray Mattson, and Teresa would soon attend Baylor University. Our two youngest, Trina and Tim were in high school and middle school. They acclimated well to a very different lifestyle and thrived in their new environment.

My biggest complaint was the heat and smog. Dick helped me survive that summer of '78 by taking me to Lancaster, Pennsylvania, countryside several times where I could see blue skies and breathe clean air!

After about six or eight months working at the Pentagon, General Jones spoke to me about broadening my duties. "Dick, would you take on the additional responsibility of working the 'people side' of the Hill? Not by tracking legislation, but by being my interface with members of Congress? Go with me to the hearings and build relationship with congressional members and staff."

General Jones had three attorneys who were his "legislative people," but he explained how he needed someone who knew how to work with people, one who would handle his public speaking, appearance schedules, and the community relations activities as well as accompanying him to the Hill during congressional hearings. I would oversee all press activities as well as any interaction with members of Congress.

The organizational chart for the Joint Chiefs of Staff of 1979 identified me as "Public Affairs." However, my working title was Special Assistant to the Chairman of the Joint Chiefs of Staff. Besides traveling with General Jones most of the time, I stayed in contact with the service, legislative staff as well as the Department of Defense. It was a challenging job at times. General Jones told me, "You know there is no job description for what I'm asking you to do. You seek your own level of involvement."

Working with General Jones was a wonderful experience but a tremendous learning curve. That was my seventh and eighth year of doing service working with the leadership of all military branches. I have often thought that I probably should have never become a general in the Air Force later with that much unified service. Anyway, it was a great period, being on the inside where global military decisions were made.

In 1978, the world was stunned to learn that fifty-two American diplomats and citizens were taken hostage after a group of Iranian students took over the US embassy in Teheran. Their goal was to force the United States to hand over the deposed Shah of Iran who was being treated for cancer here in the United States. They wanted him returned so he could be tried and executed for "crimes committed during his reign." Of course, President Carter wisely countered, "We will not give in to blackmail."

It was the middle of the night in April 1980 when I received a call from General Jones. There was concern and urgency in his voice, "Dick, I need you down here right away." I dressed and twenty minutes later was standing in his office in the Pentagon.

"We just tried to rescue the prisoners from Teheran, and it broke."

By "broke," he meant that it had failed.

I knew that negotiations to acquire the prisoners' release from Teheran had been ongoing for months, and now the general was telling me that the US military attempted a rescue operation the night before under the code name "Operation Eagle Claw," with the USS Nimitz and USS Coral Sea involved in the operation. The results however had been a complete debacle. Most disturbing was the news that the aborted rescue mission left eight American servicemen dead.

I didn't know the full scoop until the next day. My first instruction from General Jones was to meet with General PX Kelly, who was over the Joint Chiefs of Staff Operations (JCS/Ops) and also with Tom Ross, the assistant secretary of Defense for Public Affairs. "You and Tom are to be the principal spokesmen," Jones said.

It was a challenging few hours because information had been so tightly held that only a handful of people, including the President, knew the complete details of the rescue attempt. I certainly was unaware of the operation. Later, many said, "Dick, you should have known about it." However, I actually was protected by not knowing about the operation. The general was wise in not giving us the word beforehand.

I do recall a couple of incidents that should have drawn my attention to the upcoming mission. Marine Colonel Pittman was a good friend and was part of the four-member (one from each service) of the chairman's staff group. I noticed he was away a lot in the days before the attempt, in and out, and he couldn't tell me what he was doing. In addition, another acquaintance who was in the same Bible study group I attended at the Pentagon was on an extended classified temporary duty. I learned later he was the weather information contact for the mission. There were other times I'd arrive at 6:00 or 6:30 in the morning to see the chairman with a roll of maps and documents under his arm headed for a meeting in the classified area. I knew something must be going on but didn't know what it could be. I even recall asking him once, "Hey, what's going on?"

"I can't tell you now," was the chairman's reply.

The White House announced news of the failed rescue operation at 1:00 a.m. on the following day. Before our own press briefing, we made sure we understood the supposed roles of each military service in the failed operation and reviewed the facts before we faced the press. Walking down the hall of the Pentagon for the first press conference we were joined by Special Forces chief, Colonel Beckwith, who seemed jumpy as a cat. Here's Beckwith, a tough-as-nails guy, known for being a man of steel, yet he was visibly uptight.

"You afraid of the press?" I asked Beckwith as we walked.

He answered, "Dick, I'm very good at Special Forces, but I'm not very good at doing a press conference."

I said, "Well, if you're going off on the wrong track, I'll let you know to stop. Just watch me—you'll know." Colonel Beckwith was a good guy, a real American hero.

We delivered as much information as we could that day, because some of it was still protected, and probably still is today. The press briefing was uneventful.

An extensive investigation followed, headed by Admiral James L. Holloway III, the chief of Naval Operations. The Holloway Report cited the rescue failed due to "deficiencies in mission planning, command and control, and inter-service operability." The report explained how the miscalculation of fueling needs, eyes on the ground, and problems with desert sand and weather led to the call to abort the mission.

The report also confirmed another area of concern. It was clear that only six helicopters (out of eight) would be able to land on the projected site in the desert. One of the helicopters, Bluebeard 3, needed to be moved from behind one of the EC-130s in the operation. Since it couldn't be moved by ground taxi, it had to be moved by hover taxi (meaning flying a short distance at low speed and altitude). An Air Force combat controller tried to direct the maneuver but was blasted by desert sand being swirled up by the rotor, so he tried to back away. Observing this, the pilot aboard Bluebeard 3 moved forward thinking he needed to maintain the same distance, resulting in a crash into an EC-130.

The resulting explosion killed eight US servicemen: three of the five Marine aircrew in the RH-53 and five of fourteen Air Force aircrew in the EC-130. In the frantic attempt to evacuate, the remaining helicopter crews boarded the other EC-130s, abandoning five mostly intact RH-53 aircraft, which were later retrieved and used by the Iranian army.

The Holloway Report also served as a catalyst to revamp the Department of Defense in some areas. The services' failure to work together productively led to the creation of the United States Special Operations Command (USSOCOM), whereby each service would have its own special operations forces under USSOCOM's direct overall control.

The initial rescue plan had some great validity, but a couple of unforeseen things happened. The following is my own opinion as to why the rescue mission failed. First, they put Marine helicopters on the carriers and not Air Force helicopters, because the Marine aircraft had collapsible rotor blades. They could put the Marine helicopters below deck and hide them from Soviet intelligence tracking the ships in the Indian Ocean. The Soviets would have known something was up with a bunch of helicopters on carrier decks, which were not there normally. Also, the plan called for Marine pilots, and in retrospect, they probably needed Air Force "Jolly Green Giant" choppers and pilots because they had more experience at rescue missions.

At the time, night vision hadn't been used all that much, and the mission was one of the first night vision operations. This caused some confusion. And then, there was the dust storm, just one of those freak things that occurred when according to the best weather people, there was less than one percent chance for that storm. The weather had been tracked for six to eight months because there were no existing records, no Iranian weather service to get information. Another interesting but head-scratching event occurred regarding the desert road to be used. Again, the area was observed for months, and the road appeared to have no traffic, nothing. But on the night of the attempt, a car and then a bus full of people happened by, and they had to be stopped. Those kinds of things occurred that couldn't have been planned for.

Some said that the mission to free the hostages was too classified. Those involved knew about their part only and didn't have an overall knowledge of the complete plan. The people who knew the entire yardstick of the operation numbered less than twelve, but to me, this was necessary to reduce leaks to the media or to Congress. Remember, lives were at stake. The Iranians could have killed the hostages if word got out of a rescue attempt or they could have moved the hostages to many locations making it extremely difficult to complete a rescue operation.

Tom Ross and I were really surprised by some strange queries that would be raised by the press at times. We determined they were coming mainly from Congressional personnel. Because Congress was not privy to the details of the highly classified failed mission, some members were upset about being out of the loop. Then, also, the press didn't have details, which frustrated them, so they went to their contacts and came up with all kinds of inaccurate theories. In efforts to save credibility, they would ask questions citing "an informed source" or made guesses as to what could have occurred. Some of the questions and concerns were really off-the-wall stuff.

General Jones would eventually sit through over one hundred hours of congressional hearings on the rescue attempt. The Department of Defense had their press briefings and were conducting them twice a week for a time.

I know a lot would have happened differently if we had great twenty-twenty hindsight, but all in all, I thought General Jones and the team did a great job. General PX Kelly was marvelous to work with, and Tom Ross was a real champion; I have a tremendous amount of respect for him.

Of course, the sad and frustrating result of the failed rescue attempt was that the American hostages were indeed subsequently dispersed and scattered to various locations through out the country, making a second attempt for rescue improbable. Finally, after being held for 444 days, the hostages were released in January of 1981 after Ronald Reagan became president. Jimmy Carter has stated that the aborted mission to retrieve our people cost him the reelection. I don't personally believe it was the *only* reason, but the event certainly didn't help his bid for a second term.

I am proud of the way General Jones handled the spotlight and led our office to make sure of all facts in order to answer questions from the media. He also made himself available to Congress for hours of testimony related to the botched rescue, all the while offering and maintaining an attitude of full disclosure whenever possible. It was a learning experience like no other as I observed and participated in the inner workings of our government and its military forces in the face of such a disaster. In the coming months, I would have to deal with other tragic circumstances that demanded tough scrutiny and changes in procedures.

~ 11 ~

Covering Tragic Events Just Part of the Job

By 1980, Ann and I were already thinking about retiring after my time with the Chairman of the Joint Chiefs of Staff. The Chiefs of Staff of each service are appointed to terms of four years, the chairman for two years. The Chairman may then be selected for another two years, but that is the term limit.

One interesting side note, General Jones who came in under President Carter was indeed renominated for a second two-year term to serve the new president, Ronald Reagan. However, a controversy arose regarding his appointment.

Tim, our fourteen-year-old son, happened to be a summer Senate page when General Jones came up for re-appointment. One night around 10:00 p.m., Tim called from the Capitol and said, "Dad, you better get down here. They are discussing General Jones's nomination." I departed immediately for DC.

I spoke with Bill Armstrong, the Colorado United States Senator, after arriving at the capitol. He explained to me how one particular senator was opposing the general's nomination because the general had backed Carter's decision to cancel the B-1 bomber.

General Jones had earlier written a letter to Senator John Stennis, chairman of the Senate Armed Services Committee, after being informed President Carter had cancelled the B-1. In essence, the letter stated, "It is my opinion that it (the B-1) is a valuable instrument. However, the president's position is what we abide by, because we are under civilian control." He also informed the Air Force, "We are not going to back-door the president. That is not what we are here to do."

Jones was right, but he almost missed the opportunity to serve the additional term due to that issue. There were many who had worked on the B-1 who continued to feel it was a necessary system, and there were advocates for its relevancy in a lot of different venues. I don't believe there was a concerted effort to promote the B-1 after it was cancelled.

In 1980, General Jones was eventually reappointed for two more years, and I thought, "Well, I'll spend two more years here, which fits with the family phasing, kids in school, etc. Then I'll retire when my boss retires." Anyway, that became the joke between us, that I had been extended for two more years also. He and I laughed about it. "I recognize I serve at the pleasure of the Chairman," I said.

"Oh, don't worry," he told me. Then, two weeks later, he called and said, "Dick, you need to go upstairs and talk to the Secretary of the Air Force. They want to talk to you about being the next Director of Public Affairs."

That was not in my plan, and I had never even thought about being in that position but was scheduled for an interview with Secretary of the Air Force, Hans Mark, and also with General Lew Allen, who was Air Force Chief at that time. I was informed shortly thereafter that I had been appointed as the new Director of Public Affairs for the Air Force.

As stated, I was ready to retire as a colonel but realized there had been some problems with the Air Force relating to the press, so I remained in order to accept the new challenge. It has always been my opinion that you may not like the press, but you must work with them. In order for the Air Force to tell its story, we needed the "publics" of the world, and especially those in our own country, to help us tell the story.

General Jerry Dalton was a strong, effective professional public affairs director highly respected by the public affairs community. My new team reflected his training, which I always appreciated.

One of the first things we did was schedule an interview with a television station about various upcoming military projects. The interview went well as Dr. Mark, the Air Force Secretary, tried to keep the information as nontechnical as he could. At one point, they unplugged the microphones and wanted to shoot over Dr. Mark's shoulder for a cutaway shot of the correspondent, a common technique used to put together a show with only one camera in use.

To capture the shot, the correspondent and Dr. Mark were chitchatting about nothing really, so the camera could catch the participants with their lips moving but no sound. Suddenly, the correspondent asked, "We really spend a lot of money on the space program. Is it really worth it?"

Dr. Mark replied, "Well, sometimes you do it just for the hell of it."

Not missing a beat, the correspondent said, "Can I get that on tape?"

"No!" I emphatically said from where I was standing to the side.

"Why not?" Dr. Mark said looking at me with a straight face.

I said, "Well, imagine that some guy comes in from grabbing a beer, and all he hears is that one comment. He thinks, 'Hey, the Secretary of the Air Force says we spend money on space just for the heck of it.'"

I knew Dr. Mark didn't fully agree, but he went along with my decision. He didn't say anything further, and I escorted the media guys from the office.

That night Dr. Mark and I happened to be leaving the Pentagon at the same time. As I came down the escalator, Dr. Mark was coming down the stairs. We walked toward the rear entrance together, and he said, "Well, Dick, I thought you were going to be a lot of fun to work with as a PA [Public Affairs], but you know, you're pretty stuffy."

I'll never forget that. We actually had a wonderful relationship, and I appreciated Dr. Mark very much. He was a brilliant man, a nuclear physicist who designed the Pioneer spacecraft.

On a much more serious note, disaster struck on September 19, 1980, when a Titan missile exploded in the launch duct just outside the small Arkansas town of Damascus. Some may recall that the site, Titan II Launch Complex 374-7, had already experienced a disaster in 1978 when a leak from an oxidizer sent toxic fumes three thousand feet long, three hundred feet wide, and one hundred feet high drifting across US Highway 65. Many were evacuated from the area, and a few people were taken ill, but the leak was very quickly repaired. The 1980 incident that followed would not be as simple to handle.

The cause for the explosion could not have been anticipated. The day before the explosion around 6:30 p.m. while conducting maintenance on the missile, an airman unfortunately dropped a wrench socket. The tool fell eighty feet before hitting the rocket's first-stage fuel tank, causing a hole in the tank, which began to leak. By 9:00 p.m., the Air Force began to evacuate personnel and nearby residents while trying to determine the status and elements of danger the missile posed.

In the early hours of the next morning, September 19, Senior Airman David Livingston and Sergeant Jeff K. Kennedy entered the launch complex to check the airborne fuel concentrations and found them to be alarming, at their maximum. After the readings, around 3:00 a.m., the two men were sitting on the concrete edge near the missile when it exploded sending the 740-ton launch duct closure door two hundred feet in the air and some six hundred feet to the northeast of the complex.

Landing 100 feet from the entry gate to the complex was the W-53 nuclear warhead. Thankfully its safety features prevented loss of radioactive material, but both men were injured. Kennedy's leg was broken when he was blown 150 feet from the silo. Security found Livingston under the rubble of the launch duct and evacuated him, but he died hours later. Twenty-one people were hurt by the explosion directly or during rescue attempts.

Tons of debris were collected over an area of four hundred acres surrounding the missile site, and thousands of gallons of contaminated water had to be pumped from the silo. As you can imagine, it was a mess. The total cost to replace the complex was close to $225 million and another $20 million for cleanup costs. We (the Air Force) decided it was best to seal the entire complex.

Of course, a congressional inquiry found that the Titan II program was basically reliable but determined better communication was needed between local officials and the Air Force in regard to potential accidents. The policy of the Air Force had been to neither confirm or deny the presence of nuclear weapons at an accident site. This policy would be modified in the future due to the potential harm to the civilian population. In 2000, the Titan II Missile Complex 374-7 was listed in the National Register of Historic Places.

Due to the incident, I would spend a lot of time reassuring the public through the press, trying to relay correct information and calm the public's fear of other missile sites.

September 1980 was a challenging month for the Air Force from a public relations standpoint, and I was new on the job. A few days before the Titan incident in Arkansas, a B-52 wing fire at Grand Forks Air Force Base in Dakota was a potential catastrophe too. Only a wind coming from the southwest kept a nuclear disaster at bay. The *Chicago Tribune* reported that the wing fire "burned like a blow torch for three hours."

The B-52 carried thermonuclear weapons so if the wing fire had expanded to reach the weapons, it could have resulted in a nuclear explosion affecting a sixty-square-mile area in Minnesota and North Dakota and thousands of people living near the air base.

Our salvation was the steady and strong twenty-six-mile-per-hour wind blowing away from the bomb bay. We watched that closely in case there was a shift in the wind, but the fire finally went out when the wing tank was out of fuel. There would be a Senate hearing regarding the incident, and eventually, the Air Force removed nuclear missiles from B-52s because of such a risk. In my opinion, our press corps did a good job handling the public attention and concern. The Air Force monitored the situation moment to moment. Folks in the Grand Forks area insist that the fire was a close brush that could have led to a nuclear disaster.

We had barely recovered from handling the public affairs challenges from those two serious incidents when a Boeing EC-135 crashed on May 6, 1981. All seventeen crew members and four passengers on board the aircraft were killed. The plane left Wright-Patterson Air Force Base in Ohio on a training mission when for no explained reason the aircraft pitch trim was moved to the full nose-down position causing the plane to suddenly pitch over. The plane became uncontrollable due to the loss of electrical power and exploded at about 1,500 feet near Walkersville, Maryland.

Complicating the investigation into the crash was the fact that two Air Force wives were aboard the flight, one actually seated in the left pilot seat. The aircraft commander occupied the right pilot seat, and his wife sat to his left. The flight was part of a special "spouse incentive" ride for wives of crew members. Since then, the Air Force has limited such flights on fighter jets and certainly prohibited civilians from having access to the controls.

It was concluded that most likely the aircraft's pitch-over was caused when the pilot's wife inadvertently activated the trim stabilizer switch located on the left pilot's control wheel. The pilot would only have approximately eight seconds to correct the pitch-over situation. After that, the pitch angle was more than thirty degrees nose-down, and the speed of the plane was around 350 knots. We will never know why the recovery was delayed. The ensuing explosion resulted in the catastrophic break up of the aircraft.

From a press standpoint, we were very upfront with the details as we knew them. The earlier you can show or explain to the media what happened, the faster you control or kill the story. We worked very hard with the investigators and were able to bring in the trim motor and screw for the trim tab for the press to view, which was shown to be in full-down position. We gave them a full picture of a scenario in which the trim was full forward. If the pilot in the right seat didn't know it until too late, he couldn't have pulled the plane back. The plane basically was headed straight into the ground. A tragic thing to happen, but I thought we handled it as well as possible.

Just to be clear, all of the above incidents occurred during my first six months on the job. I remember saying, "Boy, I hope the rest of my tour isn't like this!" Unfortunately, there would be other tragic events before my tenure was over.

Our department also handled press related to Leonard Matlovich, the decorated Vietnam War veteran who became the first gay service member to fight the military ban on gays. In 1975, he "outed" himself and began his attempt to stay in the Air Force. His case resulted in heavy press coverage including his picture on the cover of *Time* magazine. There were many hearings and the Air Force had to deal with ongoing related media interest until Matlovich's death from HIV/AIDS in 1988.

Although it was an Air Force issue, the Matlovich case transcended all the services, so we worked that one specifically with the Department of Defense, because it had national interest. It was a personnel issue, much like the yarmulke issue back in 1975. In that case, a Jewish man challenged the Air Force's uniform code by insisting on wearing the skullcap worn by Orthodox Jewish men. We realized such issues were beyond being just Air Force matters. The Air Force was the target, but such personnel causes crossed all military services and were national interest stories.

Issues on personnel usually went to the Department of Defense; however, our staff created coordinated statements or positions to present to the Defense department to help determine correct responses. And other services needed to know what we were going to say before making statements of their own.

In January of 1982, we had to address the public's need for information regarding another tragic accident. The public affairs office of the Air Force does the scheduling for the Thunderbirds, the air demonstration squadron team that thrills thousands at shows across the country each year. The T-Birds as well as the Navy Blue Angels and the Army Golden Knights have all schedules completed well in advance. We handled the annual schedule for the Thunderbirds because we also coordinated schedules with The Blue Angels and the Golden Knights with the Department of Defense. I had led the Warhawk demonstration team early in my career and also flew on occasion in the F-4, the F-111, the F-15, F-16 and had flown a practice show with The Thunderbirds.

There had been a prior Thunderbird accident, which occurred when a flock of seagulls were ingested into the engine on a takeoff, causing an aircraft to crash near Cleveland, Ohio. We responded to the media in that regard, but a worse accident was yet to come.

The Thunderbirds squad is based out of Nellis Air Force Base in Nevada. On a January day, the team was doing practice maneuvers at Indian Springs Air Force Auxiliary Field, preparing for a scheduled performance in Arizona. The pilots were practicing the four-plane line abreast loop. The common procedure was for the aircrafts to climb several thousand feet side by side before making a loop descending at a great rate of speed (400 mph). The planes are to level off at about one hundred feet after the rapid descent. Theories still circulate as to why the four planes hit the desert floor almost simultaneously, killing all four Thunderbird pilots.

We were stunned by the news of the worst crash in the twenty-eight-year history of the Air Force aerial demonstration team. Residents described the earth-shaking explosion as horrific, and wreckage from the crash was spread across a one-square mile area of the desert just north of Las Vegas. An aerial photo showed what looked like four burned-out matches on the desert floor. This was the same team I flew a practice mission with earlier.

Initial reports indicated the lead pilot may have misjudged his altitude or speed, and the other three pilots, true to their training, simply followed him straight into the ground, not breaking formation. Later, investigations by the Air Force concluded that the crash was due to a jammed stabilizer on the lead jet.

My personal take on the accident is that it was in part due to pilot error. When the lead pilot realized he couldn't pull out of the dive, he should have called for others to pull out, or punch out! They all had rocket seats and possibly could have survived, but it was tragic no matter the cause. One eyewitness stated, "It happened so fast, I couldn't tell you if one hit first. It looked like all of them hit at the same time."

There were some changes following the Thunderbirds "Line Abreast Crash." First, Congress passed a resolution stating their "strong support for the continuation of the Thunderbirds program," but for that year, their flight season was cancelled in order to rebuild a team. Secondly, the Thunderbirds would go back to using the front-line F-16 jet fighters, instead of the T-38s. Then, lastly, the maneuver calling for a line abreast formation is not attempted any longer, due to the potential danger.

The following May, a detailed five-page report of the crash appeared in the *Aviation Week and Space Technology Magazin*e. We were all happy to see the Thunderbirds program rebuilt, and in early 1983, eighteen months after the tragedy, the squad took to the skies to thrill appreciative crowds once more and to help Air Force recruiting efforts.

Even the best spokesperson has difficulty reporting details to the media in such tragic circumstances, especially when they all occur back-to-back in a short span of time. I am proud of the way our very professional staff handled and responded to that series of serious incidents.

Along with informing and assisting the media in such incidents, I wanted to build relationships with the Air Force Deputy Chiefs of Staff (DCS) and the commanders of major Air Force commands. I made it a point to call on every commander to let them know who I was. I believe my personal flight experience helped my credibility with the officers. I not only had wings, but I had army jump wings. With over 1,500 hours of flying time, I had flown jets and led an outstanding acrobatic team. That background helped to establish strong rapport.

Staff wise, I put people in place who would help service the DCSs, the Chief and Vice Chief, and the Secretary and Undersecretary, Edward C. "Pete" Aldridge. Pete was a public guy, a political appointee, and he understood press matters. He'd been around the block a few times. I placed Tom Halbert, a civilian Assistant Director of Public Affairs, with the Secretary. I was primary, and Tom was my backup. In addition, I placed Colonel Bud Rothgeb with the Vice Chief of Staff at that time, General Robert "Bob" Mathis. The personal PA helped senior Air Force leaders as spokesman for the service and broaden our staff's professionalism.

~ 12 ~

Public Affairs—Abel's Way

I enjoyed the years I served the Air Force in public affairs. As with any profession, you learn most from the mistakes you make. I won't say we didn't make a few, but they weren't major. This chapter will include some of the things I learned through experience.

Before going further, I want to brag a little on the Air Force. Through serving eight years of unified service and from knowing a lot of people in the other branches of the military, I believe the Air Force did a good job in public affairs. We trained staff to be sensitive to the need for good communication with the public. The conduit is the media, and you have to know how to use the media to tell your story and to respond to their questions. You also have to realize the biases of the media. One saying I repeated often, "Don't argue with a guy that buys ink by the barrel!"

I am proud of the way in which the Air Force conducted the business of public affairs during my stint as director. We had a part in building it, but the system has carried on through people who succeeded me and took over after my retirement. We tried to stress professionalism and the significance of supporting the mission in order to tell our story. Like any of the military services, the Air Force will not sustain itself without public support.

What is "public support"? It is the man or woman on the street, elected officials, and all news organizations. They need to know, and the Air Force must tell them *what* we are doing, *why* we are doing it, and *how* we are doing it.

Serving in the nation's capitol was a great time for our family, and I enjoyed working with most news affiliates, but I do not miss dealing with a few whose basic agenda was not always supportive of our country. In no way am I suggesting we do away with free press, but I go back to the basics of journalism and the primary job of the media—which is to produce good, solid, factual reporting with integrity and balance. Opinions and speculation should be saved for the editorial page. All too often we are reading news stories full of the writer's own opinion, as he or she attempts to shape the views of the American public instead of allowing the reader to determine their own views.

There will always be those in media looking to dramatize, escalate, or skew a story to make it more titillating than it really is in order to see higher sales. When you recognize these types, you must never give them the fodder they are seeking.

Following are a few of the most important lessons learned over the course of my public affairs position:

Lesson 1: Ask yourself often, "Will what I say, write, or do stand the scrutiny of the press, the Congress, and the American public?" If your action or words don't stand up in any one of those venues, then you'd better think about it beforehand. I would ask the senior leader or spokesman to weigh the possible outcomes, especially if one outcome could be a potential lightning rod.

Lesson 2: Honesty and integrity are absolute essentials in public affairs. If you are asked a question for which you do not have an answer, admit it. There is nothing wrong with, "I don't know." Admitting you don't know some piece of information is not the unpardonable sin; it is a very honest response that can be followed with, "I'll try to get the answer for you." You can comment only on what you know. You should *not* comment on something you don't know. "I know what I know, but I don't know what I don't know," should be your stance. There is nothing wrong with saying, "I don't have the answer for you, but I will check on that and get back to you." Then, you may have a statement for them later.

There are some things you may know, but about which you are not allowed to comment. It may be classified information you cannot reveal. Be honest in that regard also. Tell them you can't answer because the information is deemed to be classified or withheld for policy reasons.

Lessons #3: Never lie to the press. You can't sweep the ugly stories under the rug, and I insisted, "Don't ever try to do that." Work on the ethical standard of honesty and factual reporting and quickly respond to the role of the media to inform. We should service media the right way so they don't get the story wrong from the beginning.

I think qualities of leadership weigh heavily in the public affairs arena. Again, integrity is absolutely essential. Any public affairs person who lies to the press has lost credibility because he is going to be found out. If you always tell the truth, you never have to worry about what you have said. As stated, there is nothing wrong with saying, "I can't tell you. It's not classified, but still, I cannot tell you." I've said those very words, but I've never lied to the press. I have not satisfied the press all of the time, but I've never lied to them.

Lesson 4: If you believe an interview may be contentious or slanted in a negative direction, be prepared. Make sure the person to be interviewed is ready for any potential question from the media, especially any "hot button" question. If the person interviewing is taping the interview be sure you also tape it. Your presence or role will not be to censure but to ensure that (1) nothing classified is released and (2) to be a resource for statistics or to retrieve a document needed or to make sure only facts appear in the article. Be willing to accommodate any request within reason.

Lesson 5: Don't think too highly of yourself, or too low. There can be, I think, an arrogance on the part of public affairs officers (PAs). Some may think too highly of themselves to do a good job. Public affairs requires serving others and being available at all times. Then, there are those PAs who maybe so intimidated and lacking in confidence that a commander won't have confidence in them. You must have a broad understanding of the Air Force (or whoever you represent) and be able to communicate well on all levels to be an effective public affairs person.

Lesson 6: You learn the most by managing bad news, not good news. Professionalism always matters. It is used not to control the news but to have good people help you. Good news is easy, but you earn your pay when you handle the bad news stories. Such experience will serve you well.

For example, if you put out a first report and get it wrong, it is hard to back up to repair it. So verify and reverify; be sure what you are saying the first time is correct, or else you extend the story. If you have a bad news story, it should be on page 1 on the first day. By day 2, it is hopefully on the fifth page; then, by the sixth day, on page 27. It should be out of the paper completely by day 7. However, if you get the first report wrong, it stays on the first page for days on end. Why? Because you have continued to fuel the fire. You have not supplied factual material, and you keep adding or detracting from the original story.

The appropriate response to a situation like that should be, "Well, I can't unring the bell. I can only tell you what we are doing now and for the future. I can't comment on, change, or rectify what was done wrong. That is history. I can tell you only what we are going to do from now on."

For Air Force stories, I would offer my professional opinion but always based on the facts of the situation. Again, you must be absolutely honest. If you cover up anything, it is going to come back to bite you. I will guarantee you just as sure as the sun comes up tomorrow, it's going to bite you. You must be totally honest and factual.

For example, when the Air Force initiated the "Have Partner" program allowing wives to join their pilot husbands in flight to get an idea of what their husbands did on a daily basis, the intention was great. Then the EC-135 crashed, killing the two wives on board along with the entire crew. That was really bad news.

When we wrote the press release, I remember stating, "Two wives were aboard. One was in a pilot's seat." My staff wrote the release together. We reported the facts as we knew them and told the public we were going to investigate because we didn't really know the cause of the accident. You may recall as previously mentioned, the wife in the pilot's seat may have inadvertently hit a switch causing the trim motor to run away, but we may never know for sure. Only God knows. I reported, "The 'Have Partner' program grants opportunities for spouses to fly, just like the news media has opportunities to experience flying in some aircraft in the inventory."

Why was that a significant statement? Some of the press, picking everything apart could have said, "That was the dumbest thing in the world. Why would they ever think having wives fly with their husbands is a good idea?" But by including the analogy of giving media access to experience flying in these airplane for the experience, they couldn't say it was a bad idea—because they took advantage of the opportunity to do so themselves. The partner program has now been cancelled.

Lesson 7: Build respect and credibility with the media, both print and electronic. For sixteen years, I worked for either a four-star General, a Secretary of the Air Force, or a three-star officer. I would often tell them, "I will be your worst critic. I will tell you things that no one else may tell you. And I will only tell them as I see them, because I am with the public, and I am trying to look at situations from their eyes. The purpose is to give you the truth."

Needless to say, at times these men didn't want to hear what I had to say. They'd get red-faced, and I thought they might shoot the messenger, but I'd always explain my position. A public affairs officer's job is to be a servant to the commander from a public standpoint and to make him or her an all-star and be able to knock off the barnacles so they are what the American public wants—a squeaky clean, solid rock of a commander.

A good commander will work the heck out of their public affairs person and will listen to them. In that respect, no one should be placed between the commander and the public affairs person. Sure, a commander may seek second opinions from a deputy, the operations director, the intelligence person, or the security police. But then, he should return to discuss findings with the public affairs director. If you have others in place between the commander and public affairs, the commander may not be getting the full message and not getting the best advice from the public affairs community.

If the commander rejects their opinion or advice, some public affairs people put their tails between their legs and limp off, even when they know they are right. I just couldn't react in that way. I would often go back two or three times to further explain my position. I would get additional data or reasons to back up my PA position. I would ask myself, "Okay, how can I phrase this differently, or how can I present it so that he understands more clearly?" It is hard to say no to a public affairs person who has presented his case logically with sound data and political and public sensitivities.

Lesson 8: Professionalism and education are essential for public affairs staff. As with any career, those who choose to work in media fields or public affairs should be continually honing the craft, learning better, smarter ways to do the work. If you are representing an entity like the Air Force, you must understand the inner workings and pay special attention to what is reported in the press, including activity that seems disassociated from you because national and international actions can and do affect many aspects of the Air Force.

At a time of uniformed forces working together in hot spots around the world, it is imperative to know how each of the military services operate, how the Navy, the Army, or the Marine Corps releases information. Because the services work together as a team. The response of the Air Force to a certain event or issue should not be directly opposed to the response of another branch of service.

The days of strong parochialism are over. Parochialism is never good, except in fun—like the joshing that goes back and forth prior to the Army/Navy game or the Army/Air Force football game. But when it comes to fighting a war, you'd better be on the same page, forming a united front for all the world to see.

I believe one tour in a unified environment should be required for those reaching rank of lieutenant colonel. This knowledge and appreciation of the other services is necessary to integrate and work together successfully.

Public affairs people need to have a broad knowledge of the issues that concern all Americans, like the economy or the political climate, issues that affect our society as a whole, all the way down to local communities. Such issues also impact the people coming into our military services and even help to measure morale on our bases.

In fact, the public affairs person should be constantly working to gain more knowledge in many areas. The broader you are, the deeper you are and the more credible you are and the more successful you'll be.

Lesson 9: Media training is beneficial to everyone. I think we can all agree that technological changes over the past few years has dramatically reshaped many professions, including the information or media field. Now events around the world can be reported in real time, as they are happening. Social media has exploded making it possible to connect with thousands with one click of the computer. There are now so many ways to tell your story or sell a product or shape public opinion. The most efficient public relations person will learn all the ways a message can be communicated.

Because public image is so important, I convinced the Air Force Vice Chief to go through media training. Afterward he said, "That was probably the best training I've had in my Air Force career. The only problem is that it came so late in my career."

"That's right, sir," I responded quickly, "every new general officer needs to have this training."

"I agree," he answered.

It wasn't long before I had a memo from the Vice Cheif to give to the Director of Personnel, directing that all new flag officers be required to get the media training. I am not sure if that is continued today, but it helped to build our credibility with the senior leadership. We were continually building the public affairs team and working on the professionalism of the force.

In my opinion, there is validity in swapping public affairs and operators as opposed to having someone stay in public affairs their entire career. I also think there is validity in public affairs staff and operators having an assignment in other career tracks. Both would benefit from the broader scope. For operators who become wing commanders, the time spent in public affairs will broaden their outlook, and they will better understand the importance of media and communications.

In the same way, a public affairs person that has served in operations has a better understanding and will be more effective in future PA assignments.

Lesson 10: Be fair when distributing the news. There is a tendency to give more information or special inside tidbits to media outlets that are tied to your special interests. We provided information for example to the *Air Force Times*, the *Airman Magazine*, and the *Pacific Stars and Stripes.* My view was and is that if you give some media outlets more than others, it will be noticed, and there will be trouble down the line. They all should be treated the same and given the same information and the same amount of attention.

Specialized service communications like the *Army Times* and *Air Force Times* could run more stories and had more room for input because they carried exclusively their services-related news. Some stories or articles may only appear in the *Air Force Times* because it was widely read by Air Force personnel. Most other public media outlets were not interested in such specialized information, similar to a corporate magazine for General Motors; those articles may not be sought out by the general public.

Lesson 11: Dealing with an unpopular policy. Following my time in Washington, a policy came down from a general who told his colonels, "Wives shouldn't work. They should support their husbands' work!" Well, you can imagine the furor that caused. That may have been an unwritten policy a generation ago but certainly could not have withstood modern-day scrutiny. The policy was actually not an established policy but rather an unwritten understanding that the wife of a wing commander should be as available as possible to fulfill the many responsibilities of a commander's wife. Instead the statement came off as archaic, controlling, and insensitive, which was not the intention at all.

When anyone argued, "No, we shouldn't do that" or "We can't do that because it is against policy." I always countered, "Don't just say that. Give the reasons it is against policy." Someone said, and I concur, a problem entirely understood is a problem half solved. That is a good communication lesson; explain the *whys*.

Lesson 12: The difference between lobbying and providing real facts. In September of 1982 the Government Accountability Office accused the Air Force and the Department of Defense of working with Lockheed Martin to lobby for congressional funding in support of the C-5B airlift plane over the Boeing 707 aircraft. To be honest, the definition of lobbying becomes muddled because one could be accused of lobbying for just providing factual information when comparing or explaining issues. Lobbying, in my way of thinking, is when someone goes over to the Hill and personally knocks on every Senator's office door to try and convince them to vote a certain way. But if you are just providing facts in order to help politicians make a fair decision, it is not lobbying. They, after all, have to make the judgment on their own, based on the facts provided.

Lesson 13: Out of the loop can be a positive thing. There were many times I couldn't answer media questions because of lack of facts. There were Air Force projects and procedures I did not know about until after the fact. As stated earlier, for the most part, it was better that we didn't know beforehand. It allowed us to answer the press with great honesty. We were given the necessary information at the appropriate time, as needed.

For example, I knew about the Lockheed F-117 Nighthawk fighter aircraft around 1982. It was the first aircraft to be designed around stealth technology and made its first flight in 1981. The plane's design and construction was shrouded in secrecy for the remainder of my time in the Air Force. I didn't know any more than the general public at that point. But we prepared with the facts we did have and drew up contingency plans in the event the aircraft crashed as they trained in the desert. We asked tough questions like, "How would we handle a loss of life?" The F-117 was finally acknowledged and unveiled to the world in 1988 and used successfully in the Gulf War of 1991.

I suppose my point is that it was unnecessary for me to know about the Stealth and to make sure we had a contingency plan if there was a related crash with loss of life.

Lesson 14: The press always believes there is more to any story. Public affairs (PA) people should learn quickly that the press will always "press" for more from you. For example, if we released a statement that informed the public that the Air Force was conducting exercises in the desert in the western United States, the typical questions that followed sounded something like this:

Reporter: "How long have we been doing exercises in the desert?"

PA: "For years."

Reporter: "Well, why are you exercising in the desert?"

PA: "Because we may have to fight in the desert."

Reporter: "Are we preparing to fight in Iraq, Kuwait, or Saudi Arabia?"

PA: "It is best to be prepared for any environment or theater where we may be called to serve."

Reporter: "Why are you exercising in Honduras?"

PA: "In case we have to be involved in actions in Honduras."

Reporter: "Is something happening in Honduras?"

And on and on. I would try to answer the questions in a common-sense manner, realizing the press wanted to push me beyond the actual wording of the press release or announcement. You have to stay on point to handle aggressive media people.

Lesson 15: Covering the entire Air Force. During my time in public affairs, we put in place a leadership technique that allowed us to have very good coverage across all lines for the Air Force. I believe it was one of the better concepts we developed. The Air Force Public Affairs community are spokespersons for their command and the entire Air Force, creating an image for our branch of service. We had a talented, professional team of servant public affairs folks who affected the US Air Force.

It was my honor to service Air Force Secretary Verne Orr and his wife, Joanne. Verne loved the Air Force dearly and was a genuine people person. He was an excellent corporate leader of the Air Force. I loved working for the guy. He did more for the image of the Air Force than most people will ever recognize. Verne was an all-star, a patriotic American, and all-around good guy. He was politically and publicly sensitive, using common sense when making decisions or stating opinions. Sadly, he would need to leave the Air Force early due to his wife's illness, but I learned so much about leadership and character from Secretary Orr.

There are a couple of areas that remained concerns to me and other leaders throughout my Air Force career. One was pilot retention and the other related to marriage and family issues for our personnel.

In my opinion, pilot retention has always come down to leadership. If you have a wing or squadron commander interested only in climbing the ladder of success, he may not give much thought to actually serving his people, listening to them, and taking care of their needs and the needs of their dependents. That shortcoming tends to leave some personnel feeling disenchanted, disconnected, and even alienated. Relationships matter. When there is none, or when the relationship is strained, motivation to "stay in" takes a huge hit. Everyone needs encouragement and positive feedback no matter the career choice; the Air Force is no different.

I do believe the Air Force has made some strides in training and leadership. The arrogance of what used to be "traditional" senior leadership has given way to a more involved, common sense approach, and that is good.

The other concern is for Air Force families. The Air Force is a microcosm of our society in that we all have to work to maintain healthy, enduring marriages and family life. However, added to normal pressures, Air Force families have to deal with long separations, relocations, low starting pay, and, at times, the repercussions of war. I felt strongly that the Air Force had to address the fragmentation of the family and its effect on America's future. I think the services are doing a better job but must continue to pay attention to meeting the needs of families—the stability of the family is critical to everything we are as Americans.

My Air Force career was at thirty years, and Ann and I had a decision to make at this juncture of our lives. We were ready to turn the page and write another chapter, one which we could have never foreseen. God directed us, and we had confidence and trusted Him to guide our paths.

~ 13 ~

G'bye to the Hill, Hello to the Mountains...Again!

Ann and I came to realize that one can be involved in the goings-on in Washington every day and every night. We were invited to countless dinners, fundraisers, concerts, charity auctions, luncheons, parties, and political events nearly every day. We couldn't possibly make them all, so we tried to pick and choose social events to attend because I knew it was important to my position in the Air Force to see and be seen. However, our family life always came first and our children's needs before other demands. We also took time for FCA groups and were involved in our church.

The banquet circuit allowed us to meet many people from our country and around the world especially via the diplomatic and attaché corps. We learned much from others, and the experience helped us to do our job better. Hopefully, we were good emissaries for the United States Air Force and represented our service well.

To put this time in perspective, Ronald Reagan was inaugurated for his second term in January of 1985, and threats of terrorism began to rise in hot spots around the globe, but nothing prepared us for the events that would rock the world a few years later. President Reagan and newly elected Russian leader, Mikhail

Gorbachev, planned to meet for an historic American-Soviet summit to take place in 1987.

Regarding our family's history at this time, our oldest daughter, Tammy, had been married for a while, and she and her husband, Roy, gave us two grandsons. Then Teresa, our second daughter, married Jim Martino. Katrina, our youngest daughter, was now a nurse and our son, Tim, was at the Air Force Academy prep school. At this juncture, Ann and I began to make plans to retire from the Air Force. I was sad at the thought because I loved the Air Force and appreciated the comfortable and exciting life it provided for my family. I knew I would come to miss the special camaraderie with great people I worked with but felt it was time to move on.

When I announced my retirement date, two great opportunities quickly came my way. One offer came from the Chancellor of the University of Texas in Austin, Texas, and the other came from the secretary general of the United States Olympic Committee, George Miller, with offices based in Colorado Springs.

Ann and I made a trip to Austin to discuss the position there, but it just didn't feel *right* for us; although we were treated graciously, and the job would have been a feather in anyone's cap. It would have also been an opportunity for Ann to be closer to her original home in San Antonio, but neither one of us had a peace about taking the job. So knowing how we loved Colorado Springs, we made the decision to return to Colorado and work for the United States Olympic Committee in June of 1985 as director of public and legislative affairs. Having our son at the Air Force Academy nearby was a factor in our decision.

I moved into my office at the Olympic headquarters located at the Olympic Training Center in Colorado Springs and was excited to do my part in preparing for the 1988 Olympic games to be held in Seoul, Korea. My responsibilities with the Olympics Committee were primarily in the area of public relations, but I would ultimately do congressional work with the state legislators and Congress too.

My experience as an athlete and coach had been primarily with the sports of track, football, basketball, and baseball. After joining the Olympics Committee my world of sports knowledge was broadened as I learned much about the twenty-six sports represented at each Olympic games.

One of the programs we initiated after I arrived was what we called the Follow the Rings Tour based on the five interlocking rings included in the universal Olympics logo. I had set up a similar program for the Air Force Academy called The Falcon Tour whereby a visitor to the Academy could take a self-conducted tour of seven sites on campus. It became highly successful.

I sought to mirror that same program on a larger scale for the Olympics Committee and had the secretary general's full support. He wired the following memo to staff: "Dick has developed this Follow the Rings tour for visitors. It's not 'if.' It's 'when,' and when is now, so follow Dick's lead." I appreciated that strong vote of confidence.

One thing naysayers said we would never be able to do was to get signage on Interstate 25 inviting motorists to visit the Olympic Training Center. We needed the signage with directions to the center between Denver and Pueblo going through Colorado Springs. Well, we made it happen, and to this day, if you drive through that area, signs along the way invite visitors to stop to see the Olympic Training Center with five areas (represented by the five rings) of interest. We also improved and expanded the US Olympic theater presentation viewed at the Training Center. Of course, fundraising was always a priority because, just as with military services, we needed the public's support.

We also helped to introduce the "coin bill," and Congress approved it, making it possible for citizens to designate on their tax returns support of our nation's Olympic efforts.

Another huge success was a result of focused sales on Olympic themed clothing and accessories. As a matter of fact, sales went from half a million dollars in Olympic apparel to several million dollars during my years on staff. Quite an accomplishment. I'm sure now it is close to ten million dollars in annual sales.

I'm particularly proud of another accomplishment that is ongoing today within the Olympic program. I testified before the Colorado state legislature on behalf of resident athletes requesting in-state tuition so they could continue their education while training at the Olympic Training Center. Before the ruling, athletes had to pay out-of-state tuition, which was expensive for families already strapped with training costs. We also laid the foundation for donors to be given a tax deduction for giving to support the Olympics.

After two years with the Olympic Committee, I resigned in late 1987 to pursue other possible avenues of service and ministry. The Fellowship of Christian Athletes (FCA) had always owned a special place in our hearts, so after discussions initiated by the chairman of the FCA board about placing my name forward as a candidate for president of FCA, I agreed to be considered. I was soon elected to the leadership position, and once again, Ann and I left the beautiful Rocky Mountains for the third time, this time to relocate to Kansas City where FCA had its headquarters.

This was a particular difficult move especially for Ann, as our oldest daughter, Tammy, and her family of four children lived less than one mile from our home in the Springs. Our son-in-law, Roy Mattson, was a professor at the Air Force Academy and, as mentioned, our son, Tim was a cadet at the academy. Also, our daughter Katrina had moved to Colorado Springs working at a local hospital. The move to Kansas City made us feel like we were abandoning some of our family; however, we knew we were being obedient to God's call on our lives.

We were eager to begin work for an organization we believed in with all our hearts.

Ann~

As the moving van was pulling away from our Colorado house, the verse came to my mind that says, if we leave families, houses, lands for the sake of the gospel, God will restore these things to us. I claimed that promise on that day. Three years later, when we accepted Bill Bright's challenge to lead the military ministry, God kept His promise. Our son-in-law, Roy Mattson, Tammy's Air Force husband, received orders to Langley Air Force Base in Hampton Roads, Virginia, and they built their home literally in our front yard! We enjoyed being neighbors for six years!

Coaching was a joy at the Air Force Academy, Colorado Springs.

Promoted to Brigadier General with Miss Ann by my side.

Met many distinguished people while serving at the Pentagon – here with General Schwarzkopf.

Sharing a laugh with Schwarzkopf and General Colin Powell.

Honored to meet General Jimmy Doolittle, hero who headed up the "Doolittle Raiders" in World War II.

Speaking at press briefing regarding NASA classified military pay load.

Showing Actor/Director Clint Eastwood around the Pentagon.

Shaking hands with Ronald Reagan: our nations 40th President.

The Air Force presented me with this depiction of significant events in my career to mark my retirement from the Air Force in 1985. It means so much as it includes the POW pick-ups, my faith and love for flying.

With our son, Tim, on runway tarmac. It was the last Air Force flight for me and the first for Tim.

~ 14 ~

Leading FCA

When I became the president of the Fellowship of Christian Athletes (FCA) in early 1988, I continued to believe strongly that the athletic community has a tremendous amount of influence in America. Because of visibility, when an athlete shares God's love, they have a unique opportunity to make an impact for eternity.

For those who may not be aware, the Fellowship of Christian Athletes first started as a dream in the heart of a young Oklahoma basketball coach in 1947. Don McLanen was coaching at Eastern Oklahoma A & M College in Wilburton, Oklahoma, when he first noticed how many professional athletes were endorsing everything from cigarettes to automobiles. He realized how young people looked up to athletes and wanted to emulate them, so he began to form an organization that would feature professional athletes professing their Christian faith with hopes of impacting youth for Christ. The Fellowship of Christian Athletes was incorporated in 1954, and from its inception, Don McClanen's *miraculous dream* has seen the movement not only change the lives of countless athletes but coaches and families as well. FCA had just celebrated its sixty-year anniversary and was still going strong. John Erickson was retiring having contributed greatly to the ministry's growth.

FCA camps are attended by hundreds of young men and women, coaches and their families. I've already mentioned the school campus groups called Huddles, which Ann and I led for many years. Ann, as previously stated, started the first FCA group for girls while we were in Hawaii. Instead of Huddles, the group meetings for girls were called Cuddles—a cute play on words. Girl's FCA groups are now prevalent across the country and around the world.

Again, the move to Kansas City wasn't easy for Ann, because we were leaving our son, Tim, and AFA cadet and daughter, Tammy, and her family behind in Colorado Springs, but as always, she was a true partner and supportive in whatever and wherever God led us. We both viewed the opportunity with FCA as a dream job and were excited to begin this new chapter in our lives.

As with any other job I held, I knew the first few weeks would be spent learning about the organization, its status, the members of the team, and how we operated. I also wanted to know the complete vision of the organization and what they expected to do over the next few years.

I have to say I was not expecting my first major challenge to come so quickly. Soon after arriving on the scene, an audit was scheduled, which revealed irregularities in the finances of the organization. It was revealed that there had been a million and a half dollar embezzlement a year before that had a severe impact on the ministry.

A lot of other things became apparent in the first few months. I knew I needed to bring in some people to fill out the leadership team. The first staff member I added happened to be a very close friend who was the former football coach at the University of Richmond, Dal Shealy. He became my executive vice president. With Dal's help, we began putting together a handful of people as our leadership team.

It was a surprise to learn that the membership for FCA was declining across the country at that time, and this was a major concern for all of us. We needed to act quickly to turn that around. Some of the things we changed were very basic as you consider them today, but in retrospect, they were important changes.

For example, we had a goal of about ten thousand campers attending FCA camps. Registration for those campers was being done the old-fashioned way, by pen and paper and by snail mail. Information was being entered and updated by hand. I convinced staff that computers were *in*, and we had to learn to computerize information for accurate record keeping and for tracking correspondence as well. We saw a huge shift when we began to use technology available to successfully communicate and be a more effective business operation.

Also, as had been the case with the Olympic Committee, the selling of FCA-related apparel needed to be managed with improved access and information about the products we offered. Merchandise orders also were being taken by pen and paper with no way to track which items we had on hand or how many items were being sold. The business side of FCA soon "came of age" so to speak and operated much smoother on a daily basis when we began to computerize transactions. We started the process of having the FCA logo and trademark registered in every state to protect others from using the logo without permission.

I previously mentioned that one of the most important lessons I learned from my experience in public affairs went even further back to journalism school. That was to ask five questions in order to grow any operation: Who are we? What do we do? How do we do it? Where do we do it? When do we do it and why? Our leadership team took the challenge and determined clearly the answer as to who FCA is: We are Christ-centered, Bible-based, spiritually nurturing, athletically committed, and volunteer intense. We were responsible for four basic operations within FCA called the CHAD principles, which stands for Camps,

Huddles, Adult Chapter, and Development. Development, of course, had to do with raising funds for those operations. The ministry also initiated efforts to develop inner city programs and began to instigate outreach for women's sports, which were quickly coming into their own.

For the next four years, I tried to concentrate my efforts in stabilizing the organization and growing the number of chapters across the country. I traveled extensively, and Ann accompanied me whenever she could. In that regard, I have been privileged in my lifetime to meet some great evangelists. I met Billy Graham in 1968 while in Vietnam when I attended a special Christmas breakfast with four hundred other guests. He was gracious and sincere. His son-in-law, Danny Lotz (husband of Ann Graham Lotz), would later join the board of FCA and became a dear friend.

Another true evangelist I came to know was Bill Bright, the founder and chairman of Campus Crusade for Christ. I have often said, "If you happened to catch a ride in an elevator with Bill Bright, you were going to hear about Jesus." Bill spoke of Christ anywhere and everywhere he had a listening ear. In 1952, he authored the famous booklet titled *Four Spiritual Laws* used by soul-winners for decades. To date, the booklet, which ends with a prayer for repentance, has been distributed over one hundred million times and continues to be used to reach others for Christ.

Along with those men and others who have inspired me, I count my Ann among those who are passionate to see others come to Christ. Ann Abel is a natural witness, wise and transparent, bold yet not pushy, speaking the truth in love. She relates the message of the Gospel in clear, simple terms, especially to young people. I marvel at the insight and discernment she demonstrates. She has unique spiritual gifts so effective in witnessing.

I often had another traveling companion during my years with FCA. Tom Landry, the legendary Dallas Cowboys head coach, joined me for special events or whenever there was a new chapter starting or when we were needed to encourage a chapter undergoing challenging circumstances.

Tom Landry's career, including nearly thirty years with the Cowboys, is well documented. He had led America's team since 1960, known to millions as the coach who dressed in coat and tie for games and wore his trademark fedora hats. Tom was a true gentleman. Then, in February of 1989, Jerry Jones, an oilman with Arkansas roots, purchased the Cowboys and announced the appointment of Jimmy Johnson to replace Landry as head coach of the Dallas Cowboys. It was a shock to the Dallas community and fans around the country.

I had met Tom when I was still at the Pentagon, and the Cowboys asked me to do the chapel service before the team played the Washington Redskins in DC. We became quick friends. When Tom left the Cowboys, he became a major spokesperson for FCA. By the way, Tom never said a disparaging word about his dismissal from the Cowboys. His only comment I recall was, "I figured that when the new owner came in, I would probably be out as head coach." He was a dedicated Christian and believed in our mission. So I suggested he commit two days a month in order to travel with me to different areas of the country where an FCA chapter needed help or where a special event was being held. Over a two-year period, I could count on Tom each month to be available as I set the schedule.

It may surprise some to learn that Tom Landry had a great sense of humor. Most thought of him as stoic because of his unemotional, controlled demeanor on the sidelines. But Tom could be very funny. He would laugh and joke and tell hilarious stories mostly about his coaching days. He was also a man of great courage, conviction, and wisdom—probably one of the greatest men I've ever known. He lived out his faith every day. He was a class act in every sense of the word.

When Tom and I represented FCA at an event, like the Orange Bowl Breakfast, I would present the focus and mission of FCA, and then Tom would give his personal testimony. People appreciated his openness and homespun way of speaking. Tom came from a spiritual family but, like me, did not actually come to know Christ until later in life. I treasure the moments I had with Tom Landry. His football players would speak of him as a man of character and high integrity. They would say they learned more from him than football; they learned about life. I also learned from him. He had a great servant's heart and desired to be used to inspire and direct others toward Christ.

One of my favorite Tom Landry quotes: "A coach is someone who tells you what you don't want to hear, has you see what you don't want to see, so you can be who you always knew you could be." Ann and I became good friends with Tom and his lovely wife, Alicia. Sadly, Tom passed away from leukemia in February of 2000 at the age of seventy-five.

Joe Gibbs, the coach for the Redskins during this period, was also a good friend. It seemed ironic to me that later I would have both Tom and Joe traveling along with me on mission trips, especially since they each represented one of the most intense rivalries in NFL history. They may have been staunch enemies on the football field but were brothers in Christ and committed to seeing young people come to embrace the message of the Gospel.

It was great to get to know other athletes who shared a love for FCA: Roger Staubach, Reggie White, Kyle Rote Jr., and others, but my greatest thrill was to be involved with young people and to see many make a commitment to Christ and become leaders at their perspective schools, young people who developed into leaders of strong servanthood, integrity, character, and love.

One of the greatest challenges with organizations like FCA is raising the necessary operating funds to support the ministry. From 1988 to 1992, we saw the number of chapters rapidly rise, which was one of my major objectives coming in as president, but we needed financial stability and ongoing support too.

We had accomplished much over four years with FCA, and Ann and I both felt our time with FCA was coming to an end. Once more, God was closing one door, but another was about to swing wide open.

FCA's staff has continued to grow, reaching 1,200 in 2014 with staff members here in the United States and in international offices, making FCA a global sports ministry reaching more than two million people each year including high school, college, and professional athletes. We will always be thankful for the great work FCA is doing for the Kingdom and how we were privileged to add our contribution to this wonderful organization that continues to affect young student athletes everywhere.

~ 15 ~

Campus Crusade for Christ

I met the late great Bill Bright, founder of Campus Crusade for Christ, back in 1977 when Ann and I attended a weekend conference at Arrowhead Springs, near San Bernardino, California. From our first meeting, Bill was convinced that I was supposed to be on his staff. Over the next few years, he offered me a position working with the military arm of the organization at least five times. I was grateful and humbled that Bill thought so highly of me that he kept pursuing me through the years. As mentioned already, Bill Bright was a tireless, effective evangelist whose passion was to see the world come to know Christ.

In 1992, my work with the Fellowship of Christian Athletes was completed. The headquarters for Campus Crusade was in California at that time, but plans were underway to move the main offices to Orlando, Florida. Bill again contacted me and proposed the military ministry opportunity. In our discussions, I expressed my desire to live in Virginia, specifically the Tidewater area around Hampton Roads, not Florida. Bill responded, "Oh, so you want to be a field general and not a HQ general."

He was accommodating and agreeable with my decision mainly because he knew the location in Virginia would give the ministry the best access to military bases and to the 125,000 military people plus families living and working there. I explained that I didn't want to live right in DC; it was too expensive to operate and live there and had traffic issues. However, Hampton Roads was three hours away, and it was a different world. From the beginning, it was the right place for the ministry. We settled in the small town of Poquoson on the Peninsula, which is part of the Hampton Roads area and still reside there.

God blessed us as we served as the national director of the Military Ministry of Campus Crusade for Christ International. I was the first retired general officer to head the military ministry full-time. When I "took the stick," we had five people on the Headquarter's team. We were committed to serve commanders, chaplains, and the troops plus their families. Our offices were in the Rouse Towers in Newport News.

The job required traveling to US military bases and those overseas as well. The ministry focused on (1) working with our forces stationed within the United States and (2) serving our military internationally wherever US troops were stationed around the world. Until I came on the scene, we had no capacity to reach out internationally; however, our vision to serve the military of other nations was escalating.

We had four strong recruit locations including Lackland Air Force Base and the Marine Corp Recruit Depot (MCRD) in San Diego. We would expand the ministry to include Parris Island, the Great Lakes Naval Recruit Center, Ft. Jackson, and the Naval Academy.

In 1994, I had the opportunity to travel to Russia with Josh McDowell and Tom Landry along with 320 other Christians. Josh joined Campus Crusade not long after graduating from Wheaton College and Talbot Theological Seminary.

Readers may recall Josh's story. As a young man, he called himself an agnostic and believed that Christianity was worthless. He was planning to study law when he was challenged to intellectually examine the claims of Jesus as the Son of God, the Savior. Thinking he would disprove every biblical claim regarding Jesus, Josh instead discovered compelling and overwhelming evidence for believing the Christian message. After his dramatic conversion, he attended seminary, then began ministry with Campus Crusade in 1964, speaking, writing, working tirelessly to tell a disbelieving world the truth. His breakthrough book *Evidence That Demands a Verdict* has changed thousands of lives and pointed them toward our Lord. Josh's ministry is now close to spanning more than fifty years.

In 1991, Josh instituted Operation Carelift to not only provide humanitarian aid to former Soviet Union countries but to share God's love as well. It was for Carelift '94 that I was invited to travel with Josh to Russia. We returned to Russia several times during my tenure with the ministry.

What a life-changing experience! On the next trip, Coach Landry joined the team and helped deliver more than thirty-eight thousand boxes of school supplies and Bibles to students, staff, and military personnel in schools and military bases. We were able to share our personal testimonies and support missionaries based in Russia.

Many other such mission trips left a lasting impression on my life, and I'm grateful for such opportunities to share Christ. People have asked, "What was the difference in working for the two organizations, Campus Crusade for Christ and Fellowship of Christian Athletes?" That's simple. The focus was different. FCA ministered to middle school, high school, and college athletes while, although Campus Crusade has school ministries like Athletes in Action, Campus Crusade ministers to a broad section of communities both nationally and internationally now, including military communities.

Sunday '95—Replay

Ann ~

One Sunday during the period we served Campus Crusade reminds me of another Sunday when Dick had a stroke. February 16, 1995, began as a typical Sunday morning as Dick and I prepared to leave for church. That time can be hectic—deciding what to wear, eating a quick breakfast, putting out the dog, turning down the thermostat, chugging down the last of the coffee or tea in the cup, then racing to the car. Dick, as usual, was a step ahead of me, sitting behind the wheel ready to go.

That morning, we drove down our lane and picked up our granddaughters, Betsy and Mary, now living in front of our home, who often liked to drive to church with Grannie and Papa. Then we were on our merry way.

We deposited the girls in their class, then proceeded to our Sunday school classroom. I recall that the class was studying a series titled *The Mind of Christ*, and I was enjoying it very much. The Sunday school class was held in a room that required traversing two flights of concrete steps—always good for the cardiovascular system. Following Sunday school, Dick and I were descending the steps en route to the sanctuary for the main service when I asked Dick how he was feeling. We had both been feeling a little out of sorts, like we were trying to catch a cold.

"I'm okay," he said, "actually, feeling better."

We proceeded to take our usual place in the family pew with Dick seated to my left, talking to our eight-year-old Mary. Abruptly I heard a very strange sound, sort of a high-pitched wail. Instantly recognizing it was coming from Dick, I turned to him and saw that his face was bright red and distorted. His hands were raised to shoulder level and shaking. He then clasped his chest.

Fearing he was having a heart attack, I pulled him over to me and, while holding him, realized he was having a seizure. (I have since learned that the best position for someone while having a seizure is to be on their side. I have no idea what caused me to pull Dick over in this position, except that God nudged me to do so). The church service had not yet begun. There were people milling about, greeting each other and visiting, like a typical Baptist congregation.

I knew at that moment I needed to inform those around us of our medical emergency and that I would need to speak loudly in order to be heard. This is not something that comes naturally to me. I don't ever like to draw attention to myself. It even bothers me to come in to the church service after it has begun! I must have had a bad childhood experience or something. In spite of this, I shouted, "We need help! My husband needs a doctor!"

Within seconds, a doctor and a nurse miraculously appeared. The doctor attended our Sunday school class, and the nurse was the wife of a friend who was an Air Force chaplain. At the same time these two angels of mercy began looking after Dick, the son of a man who attended Dick's Wednesday morning Bible study ran across the street to a fire station. In less than five minutes, several EMTs were also rendering medical aid.

I was aware of prayer being offered from the pulpit, and then there was singing. The most beautiful sound of voices singing a praise chorus filtered into my consciousness. All the while Dick lay stretched out on the pew that just minutes before had been *saved* for our family and friends. Although the situation was serious and uncertain, the love and peace of God enfolded my spirit. I remember thanking God that He didn't allow this to happen while Dick was driving us to church or walking up and down the stairs or during his travels of the previous week.

Slowly Dick began to regain consciousness, but he was confused and frightened. I'll never forget the lost, disoriented, and questioning look on his face. I recall thinking, "Is this how some Alzheimer's patients often feel?" I followed the stretcher that carried Dick out of the church sanctuary and noted the sweet expressions of concern on so many faces as we passed. I knew many prayers were being lifted on Dick's behalf.

When the ambulance finally pulled away from the church, I told the driver to take Dick to Langley Air Force Base hospital where we regularly went for checkups. The driver informed me that Dick needed a shock trauma team, and Langley didn't provide that treatment. So ever the consummate military wife, I suggested Portsmouth Naval Medical Center in Norfolk. But no, the driver said it was too far away. He then told me we were en route to Riverside General—a civilian hospital. There was no more discussion; the decision was made. "But I don't know anyone at Riverside and have never felt comfortable in a civilian medical facility," I thought as we sped along.

The next evidence of God's obvious sovereignty in the entire situation became abundantly clear when we arrived at the emergency room. Dr. Andrew (Drew) Matthews, an Air Force doctor and another one of the guys who attended Dick's Wednesday morning Bible study greeted us. "General, sir," he said to Dick, "I'm going to take care of you."

What a wonderful relief to me. I knew that Drew loved Dick and that his presence was God's provision for Dick and for me. Ironically, but in God's perfect timing, Drew had been called into help that morning at Riverside. He had never been called to work at Riverside on a Sunday morning, and probably never was again. I knew God had placed Air Force Doctor Andrew Matthews in that civilian hospital on that day "for such a time as this."

Drew did take good care of Dick and saw him through yet another grand mal seizure and the complications that accompanied it. Throughout the afternoon, Drew labored very hard as God used him to save Dick's life. Yes, there were some tense moments but never without assurance that our great God and loving Lord was in full and complete control of the entire situation.

Only after Dick was stabilized did Dr. Drew show emotion. With tears in his eyes, he told Dick, "Sir, I was afraid I was going to lose you." Only then did I fully realize how difficult the episode had been on the young doctor who prayed as he worked feverishly and competently to apply his medical skills on a man he knew, respected, and loved.

Even through the serious ordeal, there were interspersed moments of humor. For example, soon after arriving at the hospital, medical personnel began asking Dick questions in order to determine if he was functioning well mentally. Most of the time he answered the questions accurately, but try as he might, he couldn't come up with the current day, month, and year. Finally, in frustration at being asked the same question again and again, he replied, "Doesn't anybody around here have a calendar?"

Another repeated question to him was, "Do you know who the president of our country is?"

After trying to process that, he came back with, "I don't want to remember!"

One other humorous incident involved Dick's CAT scans that had been sent from Langley to Riverside Hospital. Dr. Drew was very relieved when they arrived so quickly. However, when he pulled one scan out of the envelope, he smiled broadly and said, "Well, it's a very good picture, but it's not going to help me much. This one is Dick's kidney."

Dick often tells a funny story when he speaks about a test for residents of a mental ward. They had to pass the test in order to be released. The questions on the test pertained to human body parts and their location. The punch line has one guy who passed the test being asked, "So how'd you do it?"

"Kidneys!" he said while pointing to his head.

Our daughter, Tammy, and I had a good and needed laugh over that.

In the early evening of that memorable day, Dick was finally transferred to a coronary acute care unit. Up to that point, I hadn't been alone for any length of time during the ordeal. The chaplain, whose wife had first attended Dick in the church sanctuary, stayed by my side, only leaving me to get something to drink. Numerous others including friends and our pastor from church, fellow Campus Crusade military staff, and men from Dick's Bible study had gathered at the hospital awaiting word. These dear ones were especially comforting and helpful to our daughter Tammy throughout the day. Tammy's husband and their sons had been out of town at a state wrestling competition on the morning Dick collapsed.

We were getting settled into the coronary unit room when the attending nurse stepped in. She informed us that her husband also attended Dick's Wednesday Bible study. It was at that moment that the complete picture materialized for me. I saw how God's amazing sovereignty had perfectly guided us through the traumatic experience.

Dick spent several days in the hospital and underwent many medical tests, which eventually revealed that Dick was stricken due to epilepsy. We were shocked. Epilepsy. That meant he had lived for over sixty-three years with no apparent symptoms and could have had possible seizures at any time. We considered the potentially dangerous situations he had been in throughout his life where having a seizure would have been quite serious for himself and others. Again, we were overwhelmed with God's protective grace.

We have adjusted to the fact that Dick will need to take medication most likely for the rest of his life, but that's a small price to pay. Many others do the same. The biggest adjustment was that Dick was unable to drive for six months, which meant literally, "whither thou goest, I shall go!" He accepted the limitation with good nature and wasn't even a back-seat driver. In fact, he was a great navigator, in spite of his pilot training.

That Sunday, along with other events in our lives, have been sobering and remind us anew of the brevity of this life and how very fragile these human bodies are. No longer do we say, "I wonder what this day holds." Instead, it's "One never knows what each second will reveal, but we know Who holds us in His hands."

The events of that Sunday along with many life situations since have caused Dick and me to reevaluate our lives, our marriage, and the purpose of our days. We urge everyone to do the same. Cherish each day and one another—for truly, only our heavenly Father knows what each moments holds. We press on, committed to each other, our family, and to the work that God has called us to do. To God be the glory for the gift of each new day and all He has done to show us His love.

Yes, I recovered from yet another Sunday health emergency and continued my work. I was with Campus Crusade for a total of fourteen years. During that time, among other initiatives, the Lord granted us the opportunity of establishing the volunteer program. We also worked on initiating and developing the HR department for the military ministry.

Then in 2001, like the rest of the country, we were stunned by the terrorist attacks on the World Trade Center in New York and the Pentagon. I'm still not over it. I was coming out of a morning leadership meeting, and Ann called to share news of the attack. Our staff reconvened and went into a prayer mode after receiving the news. We crowded around television sets and followed for hours the devastating scenes in New York and at the Pentagon and a field near Shanksville, Pennsylvania, where a fourth plane crashed after its passengers tried to overcome the hijackers. That plane was bound for Washington, DC.

In the weeks and months following as President George W. Bush rallied the nation and Operation Desert Storm got underway,

Campus Crusade also was busy in support of the deployed troops. We put together what we called Rapid Deployment Kits (RDKs), which included a New Testament with a camouflaged cover small enough to fit in a pocket, a devotion guide from Daily Bread, and Bill Bright's pamphlet titled "Would you Like to Know God Personally?" By 2005, we had distributed over two million deployment kits, which were paid for by generous people who invested in that part of the ministry and assembled by volunteers who faithfully assisted. God blessed that effort and we had tremendous results. We also did something similar for our military chaplains called "Chaplain" boxes.

A heavy sadness came to me in 2003 when Bill Bright, the founder of Campus Crusade and mentor to me and countless individuals, died. He was survived by his wife, Vonette; sons, Zachary and Brad; and four grandchildren. Reverend Billy Graham, also a friend, released the following statement upon hearing of Bill's passing:

> He has carried a burden on his heart as few men that I've ever known—a burden for the evangelization of the world. He is a man whose sincerity and integrity and devotion to our Lord have been an inspiration and a blessing to me ever since the early days of my ministry.

Bill Bright's legacy will continue. I have asked God to give me just a portion of the unique and ever-present fervor for soul-winning that he possessed. I learned much from him about living out my Christian witness daily for the world to see. Rest in peace, Bill.

By 2005, another change of focus was on the horizon. I had come to a point of desiring more to use what God had given me in the areas of motivation and leadership. For a long time, those attending conferences, athletic or church events, or meetings where I spoke would say, "You need to write a book regarding the principles of leadership you shared. It would help so many." Ann agreed that this was the season in our lives to focus on our family and to undertake such projects, so I retired from Campus Crusade and began work on my first book, *The DNA of Leadership*, and formed my company, Leadership Is All About People. It is my firm opinion that we should all use our experience and knowledge to help others along the way. I was excited to see yet another chapter unfolding in our lives.

In 2009, I began writing a weekly one minute read sent electronically to help subscribers stay on course in their character. My second book, *Vector-Corrector*, was released in 2010. We continue to sprint to the finish line to meet Jesus face-to-face.

~ 16 ~

Growing Up Abel

Our daughters, Tammy, Teresa, and Trina have some great memories of our first assignment in Colorado at the Academy, years spent in Hawaii, and following. I've asked them to give some insight into the years they spent growing up Abel. Our son, Tim, was born in 1966, so his earliest memories come after the family relocated to Hawaii. For a glimpse into our family and the priorities Ann and I tried to instill, I have asked each of the children to share what life was like in the Abel household. I'm sure we made some mistakes along the way, but thank God for resilient children who have become great, contributing adults and wonderful parents themselves. We are most thankful that our children and their children (our grandchildren) are Christians. We trust our "greats" will be also. They all continue to make us proud every day, and they are our primary legacy.

Tammy Abel Mattson, our oldest daughter, is a former teacher, now a full-time homemaker who lives in Purcellville, Virginia, with her husband, Roy. Their children are Timothy, Elizabeth, David, and Mary.

There is a old photo of me in a little cheerleading outfit taken during a football game on the Air Force base in Texas when I was around three years old. I was too young to remember that moment, but I have always been close to my dad and have enjoyed just hanging around him, no matter what he was doing.

The earliest memories I recall go back to the years we spent in Colorado Springs at the United States Air Force Academy. I loved it! We lived there five years (my first through fifth grades). I remember every morning looking up at the mountains and loving the God who made them and thinking about Psalm 121; lovely memories!

As the oldest child, I did a lot of babysitting of my sisters and brother, after he came along. I would pretend that I was the teacher and my siblings, the students. Perhaps I was destined to be a teacher from an early age. I spent several years teaching after our children were raised. Now as a homemaker I also am a caretaker for my husband's mom.

Our lives as children revolved around the schedule and events happening at the academy. I remember seeing Dad jogging around the base accompanied by our beagle-mix dog, Happy. I was too small to remember, but we are told Dad would often take me and my sister, Teresa, along for ski trips with the Air Force Academy Ski Club on Sundays.

My folks attended an Episcopal Church for a time, and Mom hosted a Good News Club in our basement (through Child Evangelism Fellowship). I believe it was here that I first opened my heart to receive Christ. When Dad left to serve a year in Vietnam, Mom took us to San Antonio, Texas, where her folks lived. Our house wasn't far from them. I spent my sixth grade year there. I remember missing Dad so much while he was away. We were all grateful when he returned home, safely!

Dad was assigned to the Pacific Command in Hawaii when I was in the seventh grade, and we would remain there until after my ninth grade year. In Hawaii, the family attended the International Baptist Church, under the leadership of Pastor Jim Cook. Dad really grew in the Lord during that period. Our entire family was baptized in the Pacific Ocean.

Around the same time, Dad and Mom began a Fellowship of Christian Athlete's Huddle group at the high school I eventually would attend. I became close to the guys and girls in that group and later dated one of them.

Our family didn't go on expensive vacations, just usually went to our grandparents' homes to spend a few days. Wouldn't you know it, after I married at nineteen, I missed out on the two big family vacations to Australia and New Zealand and Europe! But as a family, we had been involved in FCA events together, so I have many memories from those special times. I also loved going to church youth camp each summer.

As for discipline, Dad was mainly the one who would give the spankings; Mom stuck to the lectures! They were strict, but I don't remember much grounding for me. I think I was spanked enough as a young one that I didn't mess with disobedience as an older kid! I don't recall a lot of rules for dating. I think they figured a solid biblical foundation had been laid and our church and youth group covered the topic as well. It was a tremendous blessing to associate with other families who shared my parents' ideals for living a godly, moral life.

Like most couples, I'm sure Mom and Dad had some rough times because they are two very different people, but they did not argue in front of us. We never questioned their commitment to each other, and really, that is how we show love, through our commitment. Even as a child, I appreciated the way they ministered together in FCA. Later my husband and I would emulate that involvement and be in ministries that included the entire family just as mine did. We would also lead FCA Huddles in the public schools our children attended.

The earliest example of my dad's spiritual walk is how he would read from the *Our Daily Bread* devotional around the breakfast table as far back as I can remember. I read it still to this day each morning. Because of my parents' example, I have always been involved in a local church. Even in college, I attended Campus Crusade for Christ, and it was normal for me to turn to God for needs big and small and seek His will for my life.

Just before leaving for college, Dad and I had a lovely conversation, which I remember well. He told me life would never be the same once I left the nest, and he was right. He sort of prepared me for the grand adventure of being on my own. Like his mother (my grandmother), Dad could be playful and funny too, playing around with puppets or wearing crazy masks at Halloween, making goofy faces. For the most part, Dad kept his emotions in check, worked out any disappointments or problems quietly on his own. He and Mom are both from German stock, so we didn't have a super demonstrative family, though we were told we were loved every day. I think both Dad and Mom have softened over the years and have become more expressive about their feelings and emotions, especially toward family.

If I could tell Dad one thing it would be this: I have always believed in you. Even as he rose through the ranks of his Air Force career and during all of the later personal accomplishments, Dad was accessible to me. His general's star never made him unavailable to me. Something else didn't escape my notice. He was supportive of his staff and treated everyone, from the lowest sergeant to the highest ranking officer, with equal respect.

Dad says, "The ground is level at the foot of the cross—we are all equal before God." So true. Dad's legacy will be his wonderful capacity to lead and motivate others, but I am most grateful that he truly loved my mother and each one of us and did His best to be a man "after God's own heart."

Teresa Abel Martino, our second daughter, now lives in Fredricksburg, Virginia, and is a homemaker. Her husband, Jim, is in mortgage banking, and Teresa and Jim are the parents of eight children: Katie, Abby (married to Adam), Hannah, Christina, Faith, Richard, Joseph, and Daniel.

I was born in San Antonio in 1960, but the first home I remember was the small duplex, which sat on a cul-de-sac on base at the academy in Colorado Springs. I was a normal kid who loved the mountains and hanging out with friends. I liked school but struggled with dyslexia early on, until we finally got a handle on that.

One of my earliest memories is how Mom and Dad would give each other a hug and kiss each morning, pray, and then be on their way. They never missed a morning. I never recall them arguing in front of us; they were able to work out their differences behind closed doors. My husband and I don't argue with the children present either, but of course, they are smart kids and know when we are having a little spat. Mom and Dad both were extremely supportive of each other and were a united front, even when discipline was called for.

I was probably closer emotionally to Mom. Dad was more firm with us. If we needed a spanking, he was the one to give it. Mom was more verbal with discipline and tended to lecture us about behaving well. Both were very loving, yet we knew what they expected of us.

I liked the military life; it was all we had ever known. Sure, it was hard to leave friends and classmates when Dad got a new assignment, but I think it built some good things in us too. We had to reestablish ourselves with each move, find our own group of friends again, start over in a new place. I discovered that some friends stayed with you, kept in contact, and became friends for life.

Relocating was just part of our lives, and Mom made us a great home wherever we lived, but my personal perspective is that we were raised to believe our true home is in heaven. That concept yielded stability in us as children to realize our real home is not anywhere on earth. From the academy in Colorado, Dad would serve in Vietnam and then take an assignment which led to relocating the family to Hawaii. So we went from one beautiful place to another.

I have a vivid memory of the day I asked Christ into my heart when I was in the fifth grade. On that particular day, I had wanted to stay late after school, but I failed to tell Mom. So she was frantic when I wasn't home at the usual time and she couldn't find me. When she did find me, she was very upset. I remember her saying, "Teresa, you need the Lord in your life. You can't live life on your own."

I agreed, "Nope, I can't do it alone."

Mom pulled the car over and led me sweetly to Jesus, helping me to pray the prayer of salvation right then and there.

We grew up going to church. I was fed spiritually and grew in my faith through good youth ministries and good pastors. And of course, we were always involved with Fellowship of Christian Athletes.

Both Mom and Dad had a hand in teaching me to drive, and like most teens, I took a driving course too. Along with other new freedoms as a teenager, I was allowed to date, but for the most part, my group of friends did a lot of group dating. I remember once being very excited as I was dropped off to meet friends for a John Denver concert.

Usually, Dad didn't demonstrate affection outwardly. For example, I have never seen Dad weep openly, yet I know he feels deeply. One personal letter I received from Dad reveals his loving heart. Here are some excerpts from the letter I treasure:

> Mom and I have loved you all the days of your life and tried our best to help you in your life/spiritual journey.... We are NOT perfect, but we tried and will continue to love you unconditionally. So many memories with you have been burned into my brain. I would have turned in my Star for you. You will always be our daughter and we are proud to say so.
>
> PS: Tree [their nickname for me], I'm always available to talk.

I would eventually meet my husband at an FCA Conference in 1984, and we married the following year. Then, one after another, our children came along to fill our lives with so much joy.

Dad had some very significant positions, but I think the one most important and affecting was his involvement in bringing home our POWs from Vietnam. I recall watching the worldwide drama unfold on television and feeling so proud of Dad.

When all is said and done, I hope most of all, Dad will be remembered for encouraging and influencing people around the world to live for Christ.

Trina Abel Meiusi, our youngest daughter, is a school nurse who lives in Seattle, Washington, with her husband, Victor. They have three children: Peter, Jonathan, and Molly.

Because I was born in 1964, the first home I remember clearly was our home in Texas while Dad was in Vietnam. Then, Dad was assigned to the Pacific Command in Hawaii after which we moved back to the academy in 1972. I was an inquisitive and adventurous kid. It's funny how memories can be faulty sometimes. I thought I remembered camping with the family, but when I brought that up with my siblings and parents, they said we never really went camping! One thing I do know for sure is that I loved to ski and enjoyed being outdoors. Dad would take one or two of us on Sunday ski trips with the Academy Cadet Ski Club. We also went to the mountains with Officers Christian Fellowship for a week of skiing.

Because Dad was gone a lot of the time, I grew up feeling a little closer to Mom. She was always there as a stay-at-home mom, and sometimes I think a girl typically relates best to her mom. But I always felt close to both parents throughout the years.

I shared a room with my little brother, Tim, for several years. I suppose I was closer to Tim than my other siblings, because at a later point of time, he and I would be the only ones home after our older sisters married and moved away. While in Colorado, I was active in Camp Fire Girls, Pioneer Girls, church youth groups, and soccer, and while living in Annandale, Virginia, I was on our high school drill team. In addition, we were always involved in outings and events sponsored by the Fellowship of Christian Athletes (FCA).

Dad led our family to always attend church and be involved in ministry, and we had family devotions regularly. When I was around three years old, I first received Christ as my Savior after listening to Billy Graham on the radio. Later, I recommitted my life to the Lord while in college.

There were a few rules about dating. We were encouraged to stay pure, to honor God, and to date only believers. I wouldn't realize until later how good we had it growing up in a Christian home, being in church, cared for by loving parents. I knew, even as a child, that Mom and Dad loved God. Dad was generous, friendly, outgoing, athletic, smart, and a great provider for our family. He was the epitome of a *servant leader*, would do anything for us, and was faithful to his friends and a great example.

I have many precious memories after we left the academy to relocate in Hawaii. We took family vacations: Europe, Australia, and New Zealand. A favorite vacation trip was the one we made to New York when I turned sixteen. One special memory stands out for me. While attending Annandale high school, I was crowned homecoming queen, and Dad escorted me onto the field for the crowning. I was so proud to be with him and to be driven around the field in a cool convertible.

Dad's legacy will remain relevant in the way he chose to live his life—to bring glory to God. His Christian witness has been constant, unwavering, uncompromising. Only in heaven will we truly know the impact his testimony has made, not only in us—his children, grandchildren, and great-grandchildren—but in the lives of cadets, military leaders, athletes, business people, and government officials around the world. I'm proud to call him my dad.

Tim Louis Abel, our son and youngest child, is an Air Force Academy graduate, F-16 pilot, and now a captain with Southwest Airlines. Tim and his wife, Michelle, live in Middletown, Maryland. They have four children: Rachel Ann, Caleb, Ellie, and Jake.

I was born March 24, 1966, the last of four kids and the only boy. My earliest memories go back to Dad's first tour in Hawaii, which I believe was around 1969. Those first memories don't include many of my father as he was gone much of the time, serving the Air Force and Admiral McCain (Sr.) and helping direct the release of the POWs. I remember most the family homes later in Virginia on Braeburn Drive, back again in Hawaii, then our home on Ross Drive in Colorado.

I found my relationships with others through athletics while growing up. And who wouldn't love growing up on a military base in Hawaii? It was a great place to run around with buddies.

We had great sports programs and facilities like movie theaters, playing fields, golf courses, swimming pools, and even a bowling alley, all only a bike ride away. Even though Dad was a busy man, he always tried to attend my sporting events.

Two memories I'll never forget. When Dad came home after I was in bed, he would kneel by my bedside, pray for me, and give me a light kiss. He didn't know I was a little awake sometimes. The other memory I hold dear was Dad praying for me when he drove me to football practice at the Academy. As my teammates were entering the Field House, they would see Dad give me a kiss, and then off we would go, me to practice and Dad to our home.

When he was home, Dad planned activities for us, both simple and more complex. In Hawaii, we went to the beach or we explored the island, going to various tourist spots. On one occasion, Dad let me take him out on a sail boat, but I successfully capsized the boat, destroying any nonplastic items in his wallet. (He wasn't too happy about that, but it wasn't too bad.) I also recall trips made to Bellows Air Force Base and sitting on the beach. Then, there were the big vacations to Australia and New Zealand, and later Europe. Of course, once we were back in Colorado, Dad took us skiing, and I appreciated his interest in teaching me fundamentals of the sports I enjoyed, especially football. Cadets from the academy would visit often in our home, and I enjoyed seeing Dad interact with these young guys.

Most of my memories of Dad were centered around seeing him at our dinner table as we shared a meal and conversation. I also recall his great leadership with FCA groups on a consistent basis. He drove us to church every Sunday morning, took the family out to eat for lunch, and then we returned for Sunday evening services too.

Dad was not known for connecting on an intimate level but demonstrated tenderness by kissing me on the cheek and telling me often that he loved me. Mostly, however, due to Dad's absences, I was raised by Mom and my three sisters. Dad was more stern with discipline, so when Mom became frustrated with any of us, or all of us, she would pass us over to Dad who doled out the appropriate punishment. I know Dad did the best he could with the time he had for the family, but the Air Force took him away much of his time.

I can't think of a moment I didn't know Dad as a leader. As far back as I can remember, he led people, first as an Air Force officer, as a leader for Fellowship of Christian Athletes, the Olympic Committee, and also at the local church level. He rose to the top of every group of which he was a part. He was also a leader at home too—the big kahuna. That is just what Dad did—he led. And he did much for many as he was constantly serving others.

I equated Dad's travel throughout the world with him being a leader. His busy schedule translated to me that the work he did was important. I suppose the significance scale came when we moved to northern Virginia and Dad became Special Assistant to the Chairman of the Joint Chief of Staff working at the Pentagon. When he became head of public affairs for the Air Force and then became a general, well, clearly, I knew he was having great success. I was in junior high school at that time but still knew such a position was an important one.

As I entered high school, I paid a little more attention to his rise through the ranks; however, Dad never boasted of his status or military rank. In fact, his mind-set at his pinning ceremony when he received the star of a brigadier general was that "even the Texaco man wears a star." Dad was always humble, knowing God is the One who lifts us up for His own glory. Never did I see Dad *pull rank* on others for any reason.

I loved visiting Dad's office at the Pentagon and the experiences affected me. His "shop" was a fun place to work. I saw men and women who deserved respect for their rank yet were not mesmerized by their own achievements. That helped me take nothing for granted with those at the top and to care about them as people, looking past their titles or military rankings. My father taught me to love and serve people where they are.

That is not to say that the whole family didn't benefit from Dad's status—it was great! We got to stay in the DV (distinguished visitor) suites, got to park in the reserved parking spots on base. Furthermore, his position opened all sorts of doors of experience for us. How many kids get to have dinner at the chairman of the Joint Chief of Staff's house? It was an honor to meet many of Dad's friends, both high ranking in the military and well-known personalities in the media world. Additionally, because of Dad's connections within ministry circles, I met and spent time with well-known and respected pastors/speakers in the evangelical world.

Due to Dad's ties to FCA and his friendship with professional athletes, I joined him six times for a pregame chapel and pregame meals with the Dallas Cowboys (under Tom Landry), had great seats at the 1988 final four games, and had many great opportunities to attend various national sporting events. I have a ton of memories from those times.

In recent years, I think I know and understand my father better than ever before. Like my sisters, I can also say that I didn't have a lot of time just with Dad because of his work. Even in unique settings or events we attended together, he was busy engaging others. There are a couple of well-used inside jokes in the family. One, we could be at dinner in Timbuktu and during the meal we'd hear someone shout, "Dick Abel!" from across the room, and Dad would be off reconnecting with them. No matter where we go in the world, someone knows Dad.

But you see, that is his gift—people. He engages them, helps them, encourages them, loves to see them succeed. He also is patriotic to the core, loves our country, and wants to see the world affected by believers.

Another truth is that Dad, probably because he extends himself full throttle most of his waking hours, can sleep anywhere.

Our $8 ticket to a movie is often an $8 nap for Dad. Once he even enjoyed a quick nap while driving in the mountains of Colorado. Thank God for posts in place to keep cars from going over the side!

Besides engagement and serving people, Dad is gifted at, and worked to hone, communication. Both in public delivery and work with the media, he has wisdom in dealing with various scenarios and can communicate effectively with any group.

There are other reasons I love and respect my father. He is a generous man, believing nothing he has is his but given to him by God. Therefore, and in light of his desire to help others, he and Mom regularly open their home to others, pay for meals, provide clothing, and help fill needs of those less fortunate. I remember when I had friends over, they too were treated like Dad's kids, and he always paid for everything.

Spiritually, my father is pretty simple: There is a God. You are not Him! The gospel he preaches is simple: We are separated from God through sin, but God has made a way through Christ to reunite us all into a relationship with Him. My father lives what he believes. And although he did not preach to us or sit down and teach us personally all spiritual precepts and biblical truths, he made sure we were in church and were ministered to lovingly and consistently.

When Dad was home, he led us in short family devotions each morning. I thank God for the foundation of truths he shared, those I have built on in my own life. I am also thankful Dad created many "once in a lifetime" experiences for us through travel or exposing us to people from all walks of life. However, I am most grateful to him (and Mom) for the way my sisters and I were raised, in the clarity of the existence of God, the clarity of right and wrong, the clarity of existing to love and serve others and glorify God.

My father is flawed, like most of us, and in trade-offs of life, he likely would come up short in certain areas. However, he has always been God-focused, which leads him to being people-focused. The principle of "service above self" is far more than a motto for him. It is a reality that defines him. Dad simply loves God with his whole heart and desires to love and serve people. This is his one relentless pursuit. He will burn out (or die) doing it. There is no "cruise mode" on these matters with Dad. What Dad will be known and remembered for is this—he loved and served people, he used his positions (that God established), and his possessions (that God gave) for the glory of God.

Timothy Joel Mattson, our oldest grandson is an attorney practicing in Roanoke, Virginia. He is married with three children. Tim's comments represent all of our precious grandchildren and great grands; they make our life so rich and full!

To the grandkids, General Abel has always been known as "Papa." Papa seemed perfectly normal growing up, in the same way that 4th of July celebrations involving fireworks, exploding aerosol cans, and forts populated with plastic army men seemed perfectly normal. As a result, I thought it was normal for leaders to take a personal interest in the people working for them. I assumed all leaders were accessible, communicated vision and viewed their organization as a team. Characteristics like integrity, courage, love and a sense of humor seemed normal for a leader. As I finished school and entered the workforce, I found that what seemed normal as a kid is actually in scarce supply.

You can read books about leadership (in fact, Papa has written one), but there is no substitute for knowing a real leader. Papa showed us how to view career from the standpoint of serving God and life from the perspective of being a blessing to others. This book provides the opportunity to get to know Papa the way we did and see how God can use an ordinary person to make a difference in other's lives. I am grateful for Papa, 4th of July celebrations and growing up in a family that wasn't just normal.

I am blessed by these words of my children. Charles Swindoll wrote: "Each day of our lives we make deposits in the memory banks of our children." I am so grateful that Ann and I provided them with godly principles to live by and memories to last a lifetime.

The entire Abel Clan celebrating Christmas in 2013. What a blessed man I am.

At FCA Golf Tournament with Coach Joe Gibbs and Coach Tom Landry with FCA President John Erickson between the two NFL greats.

Visiting with Chuck Colson and great friend through the years, Billy Graham.

Privileged to meet legendary Christian minister and author, Norman Vincent Peale.

Dallas Coach, Tom Landry accompanied me on many FCA mission trips and events.

~ 17 ~

Author, Dick Abel—Who'd Have Thought?

That scrawny kid who helped out his dad after school at the small Ohio appliance store near Cleveland couldn't possibly have imagined that one day he would be encouraged to write books that people would actually read and learn from. The young gritty college jock who loved to run like the wind with the football cradled in his arm didn't have a clue that he would be asked to share the secrets he had learned over his career about true leadership and spiritual growth. Looking back, my whole life prepared me to embrace a role that has brought dynamic focus and joy to me during recent years. Publishing a book was a natural outgrowth of sharing with many the principles I have valued and believed for over sixty years.

My first book, *The DNA of Leadership: Leadership is All About People* was written and published in 2009. The book includes "Eighteen Characteristics That Develop Great Leaders At Work and Home." People tell me the book is forthright, basic, and applicable in identifying leadership traits. Among the eighteen characteristics listed is Integrity, Decisiveness, Courage, Vision, Communication, Discipline, Teamwork, and Love. It is my hope the book imparts one clear message: Leading is loving, loving is serving.

It was the desire of my heart to be a servant leader to all those whom I was responsible for and to. I wanted to honor God by striving to be a man of integrity, conviction, and compassion. I am not perfect, and I failed on occasion but never thought God had given up on me; He always gave me an opportunity to correct a misguided action or decision.

The second book followed the same basic leadership themes but mostly was directed to those of us who have made mistakes, lost focus, and found ourselves *off target.* The small book can be read in one sitting, but it has a *big* message. *Vector Corrector: Is Your Character on Auto-Pilot?* is a workbook of sorts giving the reader opportunity to reflect on each chapter's basic thought, make personal notes, and write out how the principle could be applied to one's life right away.

For those of you unfamiliar with the term, the vector-corrector is primarily a system for course correction. Here's the term's full definition:

> When an aircraft or spacecraft gets off of its trajectory, or path through space, it must be put back on the right path. The location of the spacecraft is determined and its course vector (the speed and direction of its flight) is calculated. This is compared with the path it should be on. A new vector is computed that will put it back on course. The ship's attitude thrusters aim the ship and the main thruster pushes it along the path.

It is my premise that all of us are in need from time to time of getting back on track with our goals and priorities. Suggested by my good friend, George Toles, *Vector-Corrector* seemed the perfect title to represent the book's content. I'm grateful God allowed me to write books that have an enduring theme practical for every generation. As my publisher says, "A book is forever."

Besides writing, I am still speaking as opportunities arise. One special opportunity came in 2011 through George Morris who is the FCA representative and an assistant coach at the University of Virginia. Head football coach at Virginia, Mike London, invited me to present leadership training for his coaching staff. Over the next three years, godly servant leadership was part of the effort to help players and coaches develop their personal character. Communicating with staff, captains, and quarterbacks seemed to have some impact. In 2013, the thought of a student/athlete code of conduct was discussed in order to set a personal accountability standard for each athlete and coach that could help them in the present as well as beyond the game. This is a work in progress. I also came to know and visit with Head Coach Nick Saban at the University of Alabama along those same lines of leadership training for his staff.

As I look into the faces of young people I meet across the country, I realize they are entering a world we never imagined as youngsters ourselves. The world they inherit is called the information age, and we have never been more technologically advanced. But have we sacrificed real communication skills for Facebook-speak, texting, and tweets, instead of face-to-face verbal interaction? Have we lost the art of listening to a real voice, not just seeing words in a text?

Yes, my grandchildren and yours are growing up in a different world. They hear on a daily basis the threats of Islamic terrorists and see horrific images of Americans and most recently Christians being beheaded or burned alive by an enemy who swears by their God that America will be annihilated. Our own government and political leaders have yet to learn the art of working together with the same goal and focus in mind. And as for marriage? Traditional marriage is quickly becoming antiquated with couples choosing the "living together" option just so they can try it out for a while, not to mention gay marriage being supported now in nearly every state of the union. Add to that the influences of Hollywood and music that spouts racism, hatred of women, and filthy language—all in the name of freedom of expression and art. Our children will need deep faith and courage to withstand the pressures of a society drifting away from the Christian foundation that past generations treasured.

In 2013, I was notified that the Fellowship of Christian Athletes (FCA) would honor me by adding my name to the prestigious FCA Hall of Champions. As Les Steckel, the current FCA president, presented the award to me at a luncheon at the National Support Center in Kansas City, I thought of the countless faces of young men and women athletes who had been affected by FCA. If I had a small part of seeing just one of them come to know Christ, then I'm eternally grateful. My induction into FCA's Hall of Champions was a humbling and touching experience as the organization recounted the achievements of FCA during my time in office. Mainly they noted the development of the CHAD Principles, based on Camps, Huddles, Adult Chapters, and Development—a forerunner to the current Four Cs ministry emphasis: Campus, Camps, Community, and Coaches.

Again, my basic philosophy of leadership is this: Leading is loving, loving is serving. As a nation, I pray that future generations never lose sight of the principles that helped to forge this nation. They are principles that have stood the test of time and don't bend to love of self or pleasure but instead hold tightly to the belief that selflessness, integrity, and honoring our spiritual heritage are the things that keep America strong and relevant.

It is not likely that I will run out of things to do in the next few years, and I prefer it that way. I'd rather "wear out than rust out." Opportunities come each year to travel and speak to groups across the country because leadership is a popular theme for military, business, and government conferences and seminars. As long as able, I will share the principles God gave me to those willing to listen because our country needs strong, godly leadership. We need patriots, not politicians, honorable men and women who will not forsake the faith of our forefathers.

I'm aware that the years of my life are winding down, but I've never been more driven to influence those who will come after me. Ann shares this passion. We want to finish well by passing on our love and faith to those to follow. Many our age want to pass onto their children and grandchildren money or possessions they have accumulated. However, the greatest legacy we can leave our loved ones is the legacy of character and faith. That is what I want to be remembered for because those things have the potential of influencing others for Christ for generations to come.

My greatest hope for my children and grandchildren is that they are men and women of honesty, selflessness, loyalty, discipline, responsibility, and, yes, sacrifice. Above all, my hope is that they are people of faith in Christ, that they know Him as Savior and Master of their lives.

This past hard winter saw record-breaking inches of snow dumped on Virginia where we live and the northeast section of the country. But there are signs of warmer days ahead. Ann is already planning a work day in the yard to get ready for planting her flowers for another spring and summer. We will keep busy. My friend, Billy Graham, now ninety-six years old, stated in his latest book *Nearing Home* that the worst thing people do is retire too early. Well, I plan to never completely retire; there's just too much to do.

~ 18 ~

Conclusion

For years, this book was titled but parked in the hangar of my mind. It awaited my being prepared to taxi through decades of memories and assemble them into a narration of God's flight plan for my life. Encouraged by my wife, Ann, and our children and fueled by the professional help of Rita Tate, I have shared this tale of how God deployed an ordinary man with extraordinary opportunities. After all, who wants to fly *under the circumstances* when the real thrills lie in rising above them? Aim High!

Football

Leafing through a scrapbook my mother made for me, I found my first elementary school football letter. My love for the gridiron grew through high school, college, and on into coaching. God has used sports to teach me commitment, discipline, mentoring, humility, and service. He allowed me to be on the US Olympic Committee staff and to serve as president of the Fellowship of Christian Athletes. Even now in my eighties, I'm blessed to minister to the American Football Coaches Association.

Flying

If football was exhilarating, flying jets shot my adrenaline up to oxygen-free heights. Following graduation from the University of Detroit and Air Force ROTC, I entered the Air Force. To this day, I dream of flying the newest jets on the flight line. God has given me the privilege of being an instructor pilot, leading a jet demonstration team, flying a combat mission in Viet Nam, and some hours in F-4s, F-15s, and F-16s. Living by Langley Air Force Base in Virginia, we see demonstrations by the F-22s, which resurrect adrenaline in even us older pilots. Flying exposed me to gifted people who would shape my life.

Faith

Football and flying were tools my Father in heaven used to rattle my cage, proving that life was not about me but about those whom God called me to serve. That list starts with my loving God, then my wife, Miss Ann, our four children, nineteen grandchildren, and three *greats*. Next came all the remarkable leaders I've served and the folks I've worked with as a leader, coach, boss, or friend. My zeal for people mounts daily as I realize leadership is *all* about people. God wants and empowers me to love them the way He loves me.

Family

Nothing I know of can divert you from being self-centered like having a family. My precious Ann and all of our children—the Abel Clan as I call them—are my ever-present motivation for seeking excellence in all I do. From loving Ann to all of my activities outside the home, I want to be known by God and by others for doing the right thing, the right way, for the right reason.

Focus

Those who know me have heard me say, "Keep your eyes on Jesus." As Coach Lombardi said, "Gentlemen, this is a football." In other words, understand the basics. Here is one eternal basic: Life is all about Jesus, not the clutter that distracts us.

Future

Where does your future and mine rest? It is in heaven for eternity with God if you know Jesus personally.

Finish Well

As leaders, let's resolve in God's strength to live a life that reflects strong character, conviction, integrity, moral values, compassion, humility, respect for others, and unconditional love. If every life you touch sees these attributes in you, both you and they will have a rewarding flight and a safe landing.

From Those Who Know Me Best

The comments in this chapter come from former athletes/cadets, military staff, Fellowship of Christian Athletes and Campus Crusade friends and colleagues, and other professional men and women I've known through the years. I must say their kind words humble me and cause me to be so grateful that God placed each one in my life. I knew in order to tell my story, these folks, above all, would have insight into the decisions I've made, my leadership style, and into the man I still strive to be. I love each one of them because they ministered to me, believed in me, and graced me with their true respect and friendship. Lilian Whiting wrote, "To be rich in friends is to be poor in nothing." I am indeed a rich, rich man.

Orwyn Sampson

FCA leader at the Air Force Academy when I became a Christian

I first met Dick in the late sixties at the United States Air Force Academy. At that time, I was an instructor and gymnastics coach in the Athletic Department and was also teaching a Sunday school class for military families at the base-level Community Center Chapel. A new cadet Christian ministry was being started in the 1967–68 academic year as part of a growing national movement, which had its origin in 1954. It was called FCA, for the Fellowship of Christian Athletes. I said, "I'd be honored to do that, but what is FCA?"

Two of the academy chaplains gave me its history and asked if I would be the officer leader and teach a Bible study. I asked what they would like me to teach, and they said that it would be up to me. After praying hard about it, I selected a study entitled "Ten Basic Steps Toward Christian Maturity" written by Reverend Bill Bright, the founder of Campus Crusade for Christ.

During the first year, one of the Christian cadets on the Air Force football team invited Dick Abel to an FCA meeting. Dick had told me that he was not a believer then but was so impressed with the cadets and the program that he got "hooked on Jesus!" You talk about a transformation! Once he gave his life to Christ, and much like the Apostle Paul, he became an *on-fire believer* and used his considerable leadership gifts to draw multitudes to the Lord! This was much to his wife Ann's delight as she had been praying for his conversion for years.

Dick was a great example of an effective leader. Among his many gifts was, foremost, faithfulness to his callings. He rose from second lieutenant to brigadier general in his thirty-year career with the Air Force. And along with his advances in rank and position, and clearly undergirding these, was his development and growth in his walk with the Lord. He had boundless energy and creativity when it came to helping people relate to one another and to Jesus. Add to that his quick and winsome smile, a unique identifying characteristic as Dick interacted with people.

We have stayed in touch with the Abels through the years and have been blessed because of it. Dick has affected me in numerous ways. He has been an excellent role model of professionalism as a military officer and as a caring brother in the faith. He is a trustworthy friend. And along with Ann, they have been faithful and powerful prayer warriors. Dick Abel's faithfulness, love of family, loyalty to friends, and desire to serve others will be his enduring legacy.

Don "Hilky" Hilkemeier

Roommate while in Vietnam and staff for Fellowship of Christian Athletes

I met Dick Abel on September 2, 1968, when I arrived at DaNang Air Base in the middle of a typhoon that had dropped some twenty-seven inches of rain in about twenty-four hours. Assigned as the Director of Public Affairs for the 366th Tactical Fighter Wing, I discovered that someone else was already there in that position! Although very disappointed, I submitted to the thought that God had other things in mind for me. So I was directed, "Get on an airplane to Tan Son Nuet Air Base, Saigon, and report to the 7th Air Force headquarters to be reassigned." That's where I met Dick who had been there since July. I believe that unexpected sequence of events changed the eventual direction of my professional and spiritual life, all with God's guidance and much of it through my relationship with my brother in Christ, Dick Abel.

Initially we were assigned living quarters as a Public Affairs (PA) group living in a villa in Saigon. From there we were moved to another villa, protected by the Republic of Korea mercenaries who lived on the roof. We were quickly made aware that if we did not turn out the headlights on our jeep when returning to the villa at night, they would shoot out the headlights so they could identify us in the dark! It was there I became Dick Abel's roommate, and he nicknamed me Hilky. Only one other person ever had called me by that name with any regularity. To this day, when I hear someone calling Hilky on the phone or in a crowded room, I know it is Dick Abel!

We share many specific memories because we spent much time together outside of work hours and being in a combat setting (sniper fire, incoming rockets, the eerie look of flares illuminating the surroundings, etc.). It allowed us the time to deeply discuss personal matters, especially family and what effect a 365-day separation from family had on us. In that time we became soul mates who did not see ourselves as leaning on each other but rather holding each other up.

Early on I recall Dick revealing that his wife, Ann, was concerned about his not having a spiritual buddy as he was a fairly new Christian. He said he assured her, "I have a new roommate who reads the Bible every day." (I had just started a daily devotional time.)

We did not work side by side. Dick was named head of Combat News, and I became the executive officer to the director of public affairs. Our interactions were many, often on the squash court. He only allowed me to beat him once! From the villa, we were moved onto the base and lived in separate "hooches," so Dick and I were no longer roommates but in the same building, still maintaining our close relationship. Here I first became aware of Dick's interests, which he described as football, faith, flying, and family. I became an early encourager for him to write a book about that. We shared at least three of these interests in that we were both sports enthusiasts, believers, and rooted in Midwest family values.

It was always a good thing to be in the presence of Dick as we shared funny stories; he was always a joy to be around. Even when the pressures of the job were evident, Dick kept his *easygoing* nature. One of his favorite sayings when things were not going as planned was, "We need to be *rigidly flexible*."

Incoming rockets destroyed our chapel, so our place of worship was the base theater. A firefight once broke out in the street below my bedroom as I prayed the Viet Cong supporters in South Vietnam would not charge our villa. I recall thinking, "Could/would I be able to shoot someone in defending myself?" It didn't happen.

We went our separate ways after Nam but stayed connected. He always seemed to be present in my life, even when we were miles apart. I was asked to join my boss in Hawaii at Pacific Command but elected to go to the Office of the Secretary of the Air Force of Public Affairs in Los Angeles, California. Dick was picked for the Hawaii job. We sometimes connected when he came through Los Angeles with Admiral McCain (father of our current Senator McCain), and I accompanied media folks throughout the Pacific region. We mainly stayed in touch by phone.

Then, in 1972, I received a call from the director of public affairs at the USAF Academy in Colorado Springs. He asked me if I would be interested in a position as director of candidates there. I declined but suggested he contact Dick because I knew of his previous academy assignment. Dick got the job and went back for a second tour at the academy. During their relocation to Colorado, Dick and his family stayed at our home in Los Angeles while they visited Disneyland. It was the only time I recall either of us being in each others' home. He was at the academy when he was called to return to the Pacific Command to join the team returning the Prisoners of War in 1973.

When Dick went to the Pentagon for a series of high-level positions, I went to the University of Southern California, then to the Pentagon, and eventually to San Antonio, Texas, to serve in the Air Force News Center, a new agency for which I had done most of the planning. Lo and behold, Dick was promoted to brigadier general and named the director of public affairs, becoming my new boss! One of the first things he did was call me and ask me to join him at the Pentagon as his deputy. After my wife and I prayerfully considered the offer, I decided to stay as commander of the US Air Force News Center in San Antonio and work for my brother in Christ "from a distance." Soon after Dick retired from the Air Force, I retired in 1985. Because Ann was originally from San Antonio, they frequently came in to visit her mother who still lived there. I got to attend her mother's one hundredth birthday party! It was always a pleasure to catch up with Dick.

In February 1988, Dick called to inform me that he was selected as the president of the Fellowship of Christian Athletes after heading up the US Olympic Committee in Colorado Springs. He asked me to consider moving to Kansas City, Missouri, the FCA Headquarters, to join his team in sharing Christ through athletics. I said *yes*.

His reaction was mostly surprise. "Hilky, I thought I'd never get you out of San Antonio."

I replied, "You are calling me from Kansas City, not Colorado Springs, so there must be something there that is special." This decision reaffirmed to me that our meeting way back in September 1968 was God's plan to eventually have us serve together for His glory.

Our families grew closer while serving FCA over the next four years and visited in each other's homes often. When Dick left FCA, I stayed on for another three years, then returned to San Antonio to join my former church staff. It wasn't long, and I received that "Dick Abel" phone call again, asking me to join his team with the Military Ministry of the national ministry of Campus Crusade for Christ. This time, I stayed put.

I had plenty of opportunities to observe Dick's personality. He has a very positive attitude and is unusually friendly to everyone. He cares about people. He is confident, has a competitive nature but in a genuine, good sportsmanlike manner. He's fun on the golf course too—even looks good always with what we in the military call "military bearing."

Dick has a gift for making me feel like I am the most important person in his life. I think many others feel that way too. He listens! Recently at his induction into the Hall of Champions at FCA, Ann quietly told me, "Dick still needs you." He is the master team builder for a purpose. It took him a long time to get his book on leadership done, and then discovered it is never done—he keeps it current with "follow-up vectors," a flying term meaning new direction to a target. He once told me, "Hilky, you are the best leader I've ever met." I doubt that, but I believe he meant it.

Our common commitment to Christ as brothers in the Body of Christ is the main reason for our enduring friendship. Further, we sincerely like each other, to the point of being soul mates. I do not recall a single serious disagreement we had—nothing that could separate our friendship or even scar it.

When I learned that Dick was nominated for the FCA Hall of Champions, I wrote a letter in support of his nomination. Some of the reasons I listed came from observing the man for over forty-five years. I mentioned his deep commitment to Christ and his willingness to serve. I personally witnessed his influence and skill as a leader. I also spoke of his passion for FCA, how he has been involved in FCA everywhere he has lived, promoting the ministry through athletics. Everyone knows Dick Abel is an FCA man.

Dick Abel's legacy will be that of a godly man. He is "salt and light" in this world. He is a living, imperfect saint, a dedicated family man and leader. I expect a call, visit, or an awareness of Dick's presence in my life any time now, and it will be good!

Steve Taylor

Vietnam friend and professional colleague who was later on staff of Military Ministry of Campus Crusade

I met Dick Abel in 1968 at an afternoon press briefing in Saigon. Derisively known by reporters as the Five O'clock Follies, it was the site of daily updates on the war by civilian and military spokesmen. It also was a meeting place where arrangements could be made for reporters and producers to cover US operations in the field.

Dick and I both were military public affairs officers; he was a major with 7th Air Force at Tan Son Nhut Air Base, and I was a navy lieutenant at naval forces Vietnam headquarters near downtown—each seeking to get our own service's stories told. We saw each other regularly at the Follies, when not escorting reporters in the field, and had an enjoyable professional relationship during our yearlong tours of duty there.

Both of us left Vietnam in the spring of 1969, heading on to our next assignments, which turned out to be in the same office in Hawaii, at US Pacific Command Headquarters (PACOM) above Pearl Harbor. We and our families arrived in Honolulu on the same day—Dick and Ann with their four kids, Vici (my wife) and I with our first of four. We all met for the first time late that afternoon in the driveway of a military PX near the hotel we all "just happened" to be staying in.

It was the start of an amazing journey for us all, which continues to this day.

We bought houses half a mile from each other in a civilian subdivision near Pearl Harbor. Ann Abel soon started a ladies Bible study and invited Vici to join. It helped save our marriage and bring me to faith in Christ.

Like most military couples who have lived apart for a year, my wife and I had all the normal challenges of readjusting to life together in the same house, plus the added challenge of "coming home" from a war zone. None of us were completely the same people when I came home that we'd been when I had left. Vici was pregnant with our second son when we moved to Hawaii—a beautiful but faraway land. She did not go through most of the physical challenges many pregnant women do, but our newborn's colic made his first few months rough on us all. The war still was going on as well. Our Pacific Command HQ was working 24-7 to support it, with all the stress at work and home that sort of schedule entails. Late one afternoon, Vici and I were out on our patio where we often saw beautiful Hawaiian rainbows. It was a lovely setting, but as I held her close, I feared the day had come when she was about to pack up the kids and go home. And nothing I could do would keep her from doing so.

In God's providence, Dick and Ann already had seen the cracks in our marriage and were praying for us both. Dick had offered wise counsel—not always welcome—and Vici, enriched and encouraged by Ann's weekly Bible studies, had been practicing 1 Peter 3 principles pertaining to women at home. She also brought home from Ann's Bible study a little pamphlet which directly helped save our marriage and changed my life: "The Four Spiritual Laws." That afternoon I read it, agreed with it, and invited Jesus into my heart. Dick was taking pictures a few months later when I was baptized in the Pacific Ocean off Oahu. That was forty-five years ago. Our family started going to the base chapel at Hickam Air Force Base and then joined the International Baptist Church where Dick and Ann attended.

During our first year on the Pacific Command staff, I served in the public affairs plans office, and Dick ran the media liaison shop next door. A year later, I became his deputy, serving with him there during the historic lunar landing mission of *Apollo 11* and President Nixon's visit to Hawaii to welcome the astronauts home.

The war in Vietnam was still going on and would for several more years. It was an important time to be serving on the PACOM staff, supporting the war effort, but also very poignant. Through it all, Major Dick Abel not only was able to serve superbly on the PACOM staff but also made time to start the first Fellowship of Christian Athletes Huddle group at Radford high school near where we lived and help guide their basketball team to a Hawaii state championship!

Dick Abel's leadership style and experience began in mid-1969, on the US Pacific Command Staff in Hawaii. There, he handled media relations for the largest US military command with only two officers, one secretary and several enlisted staff. He clearly knew what he was doing, professionally, with prior experience in public affairs/public information in Vietnam and elsewhere.

As a former member of a USAF precision flying unit and assistant football coach at the Air Force Academy, he also knew highly motivated and effective teams of people need good training, good communication, clear understanding of common goals and good strategies, and good teamwork to achieve them.

All that, in turn, required a lively concern for the health and well-being of every member—physical, emotional, and spiritual—developing their fitness for every role they would be assigned, ensuring they understood clearly and committed personally to their common goal or mission, knowing the ground rules, rules of engagement, or rules of play, and always having "each other's backs" in the office or in the field.

Dick was also a key member of military teams which flew into North Vietnam in early 1973 during Operation Homecoming to repatriate American pilots and other service members held captive as prisoners of war. He was on the first flight in and out of Hanoi in February of 1973. I believe Dick made several other round-trips too. During those flights, he became friends with many ex-POWs, including now Senator John S. McCain III. Dick's job, which he did superbly, was to help prepare these American patriots for the heroes' welcome they were about to receive, helping them get their heads around actually being free and get in mind what they might say in answer to many reporters' questions about their captivity, their many years of "service under difficult conditions," as one hero said. Those flights to freedom were defining moments for everyone aboard those planes, including Dick. He well-told the story, starting with the international press. Their story became almost a signature piece in nearly every speech I later heard him make to many audiences over many years.

So with a strong and clear personal example, professionally and morally, Dick organized, energized, inspired, and directed our office team. These qualities served them well again in later years when then Colonel Abel served as the chairman of the Joint Chiefs of Staff's Special Assistant for Public Affairs and, still later, when he was promoted to brigadier general, directly serving the Air Force secretary and chief of staff as Air Force chief of information.

In 1979, while still on Pentagon duty, Dick and Mark Petersburg, a young staff member from Campus Crusade for Christ's Christian Embassy in Washington, DC, founded what became known as the Pentagon Breakfast Bible Study. It was a unique, weekly, early morning venue for military members and civilian government employees. They met together over sweet rolls and coffee in a Pentagon cafeteria without regard to service lines, military ranks, or Christian denominations to study God's word and help each other make Jesus *the* central force in their daily lives. It was, and still is, a needed and much-appreciated spiritual oasis.

In the military culture, and in much of the corporate world also, there is a clear, organizational dividing line between the most senior officers or executives and everyone else. Dick always seemed to move easily among one-, two-, three-, and four-star and general officers, from all services, even before being promoted to brigadier general himself. But he knew the dividing line was there and must be respected. So once he became "one of them," he created a weekly, early morning Flag Officer Fellowship in the Pentagon, just for flag and general officers. The format and menu were much the same as the all-ranks fellowship, but they met in private dining rooms instead. It provided a previously nonexistent and very welcome venue for the most senior officers to "break bread together," as peers and help "lift up" one another on the common ground of their common faith in Christ.

After Dick's involvement and service for the Olympics office in Colorado, he had two longer, more remarkable and certainly leadership-intensive postmilitary service "tours," first, as president of the Fellowship of Christian Athletes and later as executive director of the Military Ministry of Campus Crusade for Christ. Both jobs also had significantly different cultures and employee expectations, with significantly different leadership opportunities and challenges in each. Dick's availability for God's reassignment elsewhere, in early 1992, clearly was a definite and significant answer to prayer.

Dick had had a long and cordial association with Campus Crusade for Christ. He was an advisor and personal friend of its founder and president, Dr. Bill Bright. Campus Crusade's Military Ministry began in 1965, during the Vietnam War, initially under the leadership of retired USAF Colonel Jack Fain. Military Ministry grew fairly large during the Vietnam years as the numbers of American servicemen and women heading into harm's way increased. After the war, though, those numbers tapered off, programs and emphasis changed. By 1992, the Military Ministry had not had a full-time US national director for years. It had shrunk to a fraction of its size after the Vietnam War, had no international ministry to speak of, and was something of a poor cousin among Crusade's larger and better-known ministries, like Campus and Family Life.

Then one day, Dick Abel and Bill Bright met over coffee—in Atlanta, I think. Dick and Ann bought a house in Poquoson, VA, close to Langley Air Force Base, home of the Air Combat Command. Several long-time Military Ministry staff in San Diego bought houses or apartments in the area too. And I retired to join them. Thus began Dick's thirteen years at the Military Ministry helm (or as Air Force fighter pilots say, "with his hand on the stick"), with Ann close by his side.

Dick and I have a lot in common but also are different in many ways. One was his passionate, lifelong love of sports and involvement in sports as a player, coach, and later FCA president. I played baseball in school, rooted for the Missouri Tigers, and later went to games to support our kids, but generally paid little attention to sports other than that.

With that picture in mind, imagine one day in the spring of 1992, as I was about to finish my final military assignment overseas, with NATO in Italy, our plan was to return to the United States that summer for one last year in the Navy, back in the Pentagon, then retire. We already had arranged to ship our household goods back to northern Virginia. As of the last I'd heard, Dick still was president of FCA.

The Italian duty officer at our headquarters called me one evening at home. "Captain Taylor?" he asked.

"Yes," I answered.

"Sir, I had a call for you. From America."

"Who was calling?"

"Sir, it was a general. General Abel." There was a quiver in his voice.

"General Abel? What did he want?"

"Sir, he said he heard you were leaving the Navy. He wants you to call him before you make a big mistake."

Why I laughed really was too hard to explain. But if Dick was about to offer me a job at FCA headquarters in Kansas City, I couldn't imagine what it might be. So I called him. He told me about leaving FCA and about Dr. Bright asking him to lead the Military Ministry. He then asked me and Vici to join his new team.

Vici and I prayed about it, called him back, and agreed.

What happened then is a whole other story in itself. The Navy personnel office quickly processed and approved my request to retire and redirected our household goods shipment to southern Virginia. While still in Italy, we met two lady realtors from Norfolk, VA, who provided much information on the area. In record time, we found a perfect place, ten minutes from our new office, and moved. The new Military Ministry office opened in Newport News, Virginia, that fall.

Soon after the Virginia office opened, Dick began a weekly, early morning, all-ranks Bible study at Air Combat Command HQ, patterned after the one he had created in the Pentagon. Later on, at the request of a US navy admiral, he formed a Norfolk Flag Officers Fellowship, also based on the Pentagon model, at the Norfolk Naval Base. Military Ministry was off and running again. It was quite a ride. Dick's high rank, world experience, businesslike approach, and far-reaching vision found great appeal among major donors to Campus Crusade too. Early on, many stepped forward to be part of the growing ministry. Many still are on the team.

Probably twelve or fifteen years ago, Dick became a regularly-scheduled speaker on leadership at periodic, week-long training sessions for new Air Force commanders at Air Combat Command HQ. I had an opportunity to sit in on one while still serving on the Military Ministry home office staff and can attest it was superb. Those talks, of course, led to the speaking and writing ministry, which still occupies Dick today.

Dick and I had been friends since our year together in Vietnam and brothers in the Lord since our service together in Hawaii for three years immediately after that. Each of us also had four children—they had three girls and a boy, we three boys and a girl. Vici and I as parents, and all our children, benefitted greatly from what we learned from Dick and Ann—from our first years together in Hawaii and high school years in Virginia, on through their college years, and now raising families of their own. Our eldest son, Dan, and Dick's only son, Tim, became fast friends in Hawaii when they were two years old. They have remained close friends over more than four decades since. Our families stay in touch regularly by e-mail and occasional texts or calls.

In thinking about Dick's legacy, Proverbs 13:22 comes to mind which says, "A good man leaves an inheritance for his children's children." Whatever physical wealth Dick may leave behind, I'd say the *inheritance* he passes on—his legacy, if you wish—will be one of *love*, *honor*, and *service*. Dick's legacy will include:

- Loving God with all his heart, mind, and soul, and loving his family and neighbors as Jesus commands.
- Honoring God and all those in authority, walking in his integrity, and living an honorable life worthy of respect

- Serving God and country with all his heart, following the example of Jesus, who "came not to be served, but to serve, and to give his life as a ransom for all."

Our Boys—While serving at the United States Air Force Academy and later at Pacific Command in Hawaii, several young men became like family to Ann and me. Their friendship is treasured even more after all these years. They say they learned from me, but I guarantee I have learned more from each one of these fine young men.

Bill Murray—One of our Boys

I met General and Mrs. Abel during my sophomore year at the academy (1972). He was an Assistant Football Coach and Sponsor for the Fellowship of Christian Athletes. He also held leadership positions within the Commandant of Cadets area. The Abels had me over to their home many, many times, taking care of me, feeding me, teaching me, discipling me, and generally looking after me. I needed a lot of care!

General Abel was the consummate leader! He understood men and where they were coming from. He understood leadership principles, led by example, and had sound judgment. You could trust what he said and everyone loved him. He had a great sense of humor and related with the trials and tribulations of the everyday man. He set the pace and challenged you to keep up. The general set the standard and challenged you to match his bar, using his experience and superior judgment to make wise decisions for the betterment of the organization.

When I was a junior at the United States Air Force Academy (USAFA), I met the girl of my dreams and remember talking with General Abel at the beginning of my senior year about plans for engagement and getting married. He thought I had chosen a quality girl and a good future partner. My plan was to graduate from USAFA, go to pilot training, and then Judy and I would get married after pilot training, since the training was so demanding and rigorous. He listened to my plan then said, without hesitation, “Why don’t you marry her right after graduation and take her to pilot training with you?”

I thought that was a wonderful idea and couldn’t figure why I didn’t think of that first, because it moved up the timeline, and we could start living together! However, I was a little anxious as I had to ask her to marry me and get a ring at Christmas, which was just a couple of months away at the time! As it turned out, we kept to the timeline. We were married on June 14, 1975, one week after graduation, but I was asked to stay on for a year and coach football as a graduate assistant for Ben Martin, the head football coach at the academy. It worked out great because during the first year of our marriage Judy and I travelled together recruiting football players for USAFA and really got to know one another! General and Mrs. Abel gave us our first television set.

There’s another funny story about me getting into some big trouble right before June Week our junior year. General Abel held my punishments in his top drawer so I could spend the week with Judy and not have to begin marching tours, but the story is too long to tell here.

We have remained close friends through the years. I’m proud to be called an “adopted son.” I call the Abels at least weekly even today. I may be a bit closer to Mrs. Abel (who still calls me Billy boy), and I know and have visited all their children. Timmy and I used to throw the football together in the backyard when he was a little tyke. All the girls are marvelous, and I keep in touch with them regularly also. I never dated any of the girls, but they’ve all made wonderful wives for very lucky men.

General Abel is one of three mentors in my life. It would be hard to imagine anyone who has had a greater personal impact I respect him, admire him, trust him, and love him. He walks the walk, has never faltered, and can be counted on to be there for you. Should it turn out this way—I will be there for Mrs. Abel should the general move on to heaven before her.

The general will be remembered as a great athlete, a great coach, an officer, a gentleman, a flag officer with credibility, and a person who personally helped, mentored, and counseled hundreds of men and women, a man who has had pervasive influence with FCA, the Olympic Committee, and the Campus Crusade Military Ministry! It would not be a stretch to say that he is like a junior Billy Graham. His integrity is impeccable, his walk blameless, and his reputation not in question.

I am aware of at least two situations where high-ranking generals have offered to help him in his career, and he refused their help, not wanting anyone to think he was given special consideration. I admire him for the husband and father he's been. He's not perfect, but he's pretty close to it in the way he conducts his professional and personal life, and I've seen him up close and personal over many years.

Jack Catton—Another of our Boys

I first met Dick Abel when I was a cadet at the Air Force Academy. It was the summer of 1975, between my junior and senior year, and I was the 2nd Basic Cadet Training (BCT) commander when General Abel took an interest in me and wanted to help develop my leadership skills. He was the academy director of public affairs at that time and decided to write an article featuring me and my leadership/training philosophy for the academy newspaper. It was such a positive article, I think it probably influenced the academy officer leadership to select me as the cadet wing commander for my senior year at the academy. That began a lifetime of mentorship and friendship.

His leadership approach has always focused on integrity and respect for people, as he would later reveal in his book *The DNA of Leadership: Leadership is All About People*. He has modeled and mentored that approach since we first met. Furthermore, he is totally optimistic about life and his enthusiasm was infectious. Foremost however is his great servant's heart. As a Jesus follower, he strives to emulate the love and kindness of Jesus towards others, and I, along with countless others, have been privileged to be the recipient of his servant leadership.

I will never forget how encouraging and supportive he was when I came under fire for my transparent faith in God while stationed at Langley Air Force Base from 2005 through 2007. Unfortunately, an angry misguided lawyer begun a crusade to try and take down military officers for living out their Christian faith while in uniform. Oddly, this lawyer believed that military officers forfeited their First Amendment rights when they joined the military. He made scathing and totally inaccurate statements about me and some other general officers that the press enjoyed printing. General Abel was immediately in touch with me to offer prayer and good counsel to help me weather the storm and message the importance of faith in the military. To suggest that military men and women should risk their own lives to protect American freedoms and forfeit their own was and is absurd!

He has been a consistent, positive role model and an encouraging sounding board whenever I faced tough issues. Like General Abel, I want to emulate Jesus's leadership style. The legacy he leaves is proof that faith is the key ingredient to being a good husband, father, grandfather, friend, and leader, and that "leadership is all about people." To us cadets, *Abel was larger than life*!

Joe Shirey—Another of our Boys

My relationship with the Abels began around 1973 when I was a cadet at the United States Air Force Academy and became interested in the Fellowship of Christian Athletes (FCA). Little did I know how much influence he would have in my life. Then, Lieutenant Colonel Abel was the officer representative to FCA and often shared his thoughts with our group. He was the kind of person we all looked up to, easy to like personally and professionally.

A couple of years later, I was assigned to meet General Abel when he came to Laughlin AFB to speak about his role in the return of the POWs from Vietnam. I was an instructor pilot and had the privilege of hosting him. We even flew together in a T-38 during the visit. We all have certain scenes etched in our minds, and one is especially vivid for me. We were driving out of the gate of Laughlin on a sunny afternoon to my house; he could have stayed in base quarters but instead stayed in our home. In response to one of my questions on that drive home, the general spoke of an upcoming decision regarding the next Air Force public affairs officer position, which was being decided between him and another colonel. "I am content that God will choose the right man," he said.

I was astounded at his neutral attitude and knew my limited spiritual maturity at the time would not have allowed me the same attitude. He shared a passage from Psalm 75, "Neither from the east or the west comes exaltation. It is the Lord who lifts up the horn of one and puts down another."

I have always remembered that conversation and shared it with others. The words became a comfort for me years later when I was diagnosed with cancer that affected my Air Force career. I believe that afternoon drive with General Abel many years earlier started a spiritual maturation process that allowed me to embrace the sovereignty of God. Another time I recall that General Abel was dealing with some senior leadership issues and feeling some pressure from the FCA National Headquarters. I'll never forget his perspective, something he learned form Bill Bright who had a similar situation. "Keep your eyes on Jesus," he said.

During a different crisis, I was with him when we drove up to his devastated home after Hurricane Isabel had dropped 80 trees in his yard. Ann was away caring for her mother. You couldn't even see the house from the driveway. But in the midst of that crisis, or any crisis, Ann and Dick have been faithful to "keep their eyes on Jesus," good advice for all of us.

The Rudyard Kipling poem "If" reminds me of the General, specifically this part, "If you can keep your head when all about you are losing theirs."

One of the most unique things about General Abel is that he takes the initiative to meet and greet people at all levels and walks of life. He has fun talking with people and learning about their background, interests, and profession. Further, once General Abel meets someone, he is always thinking about ways to connect them to others, networking for a mutual benefit. Those who work with General Abel always knew it would be fun, stimulating, and rewarding because almost assuredly there would be positive results. He genuinely cares about people, and his love and joy for life is infectious.

For over thirty years, General Abel has been a mentor, a father figure, and leader to me. He was in the audience for a speech I once made, so I asked for his critique. Without hesitation, he said, "You went long. Next time use your notes and stick to them." I trust him to be honest, yet loving always.

I talk to the Abel's almost daily; sometimes multiple times during the day. He is like a father to me. Likewise, Ann is very close to me and my wife, Johanna. We appreciate their advice and wisdom in a number of areas. We sit together in church and are in the same Sunday school class. He has stretched me to be a better Christian in the roles of husband, father, grandfather, leader, friend, and servant.

General Abel and Ann, on behalf of all the athletes, cadets, and officers you both influenced, thanks to you both for helping us "keep our eyes on Jesus." I can still see you, General Abel, making coffee and sitting up chairs for a Langley Bible Study or boldly calling a general with something for which you had been convicted. You were always bold and persistent in your testimony and faith.

General Abel's legacy will be evident in the influence he has had on his children, grandchildren, and the many lives he has affected. I would expect his influence will be most significant in how he loved unconditionally, lived enthusiastically, and led consistently using those characteristics in his book *DNA of Leadership* and the Air Force core values of integrity, service, and excellence.

Jeff Steig—Yet Another One of Our Boys

While attending high school as a junior, at Radford High School in Hawaii, General Abel (then Major Abel, public affairs officer) helped start a Fellowship of Christian Athletes Huddle. Along with ten to twelve other schoolmates, I began attending the weekly meetings. Many of our earliest FCA members were from the basketball team at Radford High. Our little huddle grew rapidly. By the summer, we regularly had fifty attendees at weekly meetings, and we were able to raise funds to send ten to twelve athletes to FCA summer camps.

One funny story from our fundraising was during a ticket sales for barbequed chickens. We were selling tickets for Huli Huli Chicken. One of our members was a bit nervous selling the tickets door to door, and at his first attempt, he fumbled his sales pitch. He said, "We are from the Fellowship of Chicken Athletes, and we are selling tickets for Huli Huli Christians. Would you like to buy some?"

Another fundraising activity was allowing some of our young high school athletes to work as extras on TV show weekly shoots. I got to be an extra on an episode of *Hawaii 5-0*, the television show was "Nine, Ten, You are Dead." My job was to sit around a pool in my bathing suit, talking to professional models in bikinis while the action of the show was taking place near us. For my sixtieth birthday, my wife, Shelly, found the episode "Nine, Ten, You are Dead" and showed it to my family, kids, and grandkids.

General Abel has always had a knack for leading. As mentioned, our little huddle had over fifty guys involved within the first year and over fifty gals by the second year. They called the guys group a huddle, and the gals group was called a cuddle.

Probably the outstanding leadership trait I've always most admired about General Abel is how he makes the individual feel. Whenever I think of him, or interacted with him, I always felt there was nothing I couldn't accomplish. I knew he trusted me and believed in me. He has always caused me to believe in me too. This is a remarkable and effective trait that he has and practices inherently. I feel I owe the success in my life to his belief in me and his way of communicating that to me. Because of Dick, I have attempted things that otherwise I would never have attempted.

While at the Air Force Academy I had perfect height (6'8") to play basketball but was told I was too tall to become an Air Force pilot. Because my father was a pilot for twenty-seven years in the Air Force, I wanted to follow in his footsteps, but every year I signed a statement acknowledging that due to my excessive height I was ineligible for pilot training. Still, I never gave up. Sitting height for a pilot could be no more than forty inches. Each year I measured at 40 and 1/16 inches. In preparation to be measured for my last annual physical during my senior year, Lieutenant Colonel Dick Abel encouraged me to try and stay up all night to shrink my sitting height for the upcoming flight physical. I know, it sounds crazy, but his advice was this, "During the night, we all grow slightly since the discs between each vertebra expand while we lay horizontally. So don't lie down until after that physical."

At the clinic, I was met by Master Sergeant Strickman who reminded me that this final measurement would determine my flight status. While I sat on the table, two medics slipped their hands behind my neck and lower back to ensure I didn't arch them in an attempt to artificially lower my sitting height. The sergeant strained forward and peered over my head to see the results. He stood up straight and then bent forward again with a suspicious look on his face. "Well," he said, "you appear to be just under the limit. Your sitting height is 39 and 15/16th inches. That's incredible."

I fought the urge to jump up and down and scream, "I did it, it actually worked!" But Strickman looked at me and said, "You know to be certain of these results, I will need to measure you every day this week and take an average."

My heart sunk. I knew I couldn't endure the trials of the previous night for an entire week, and I left the dispensary feeling utterly defeated.

I finally decided I would get a good night's sleep and let the chips fall where they may, so the next morning at 7:00 a.m., I reported to the dispensary. To my relief Sergeant Strickman was too busy to take the measurements himself, and he assigned Airman Basic Snediker to the task. Snediker led me back to the little room with the narrow table. "I don't have anyone to help with this today. So you'll have to sit up straight on your own," he said nervously. Snediker looked at me, at the tape measure, then at the records again. "Hmm. I think it's the same as yesterday's. Let's just mark that down." This same scenario repeated itself every day for the rest of the week.

I was finally approved to attend pilot training at Reese AFB, Texas, where I met my wife of thirty-one years, Shelly. I flew twenty years in the Air Force, eventually serving as the squadron commander of the 7th Airborne Command and Control Squadron. My father, Ted, had also piloted the prestigious Looking Glass mission many years previously—and had even flown the same tail numbers. A few years after I retired, he and I sat together at the ceremony commemorating the end of the Looking Glass mission at Offutt AFB. It was a satisfying fulfillment of a dream to follow in his footsteps. A dream that may not have been fulfilled if Dick Abel hadn't offered some homespun practical advice.

Today, I fly as an airbus captain for United Airlines. I've never met nor heard of a taller pilot either in the US military or as a captain of a major airline. It is important to not be easily discouraged by difficult obstacles. Persistence taught me there is always more than one way to get where I want to go.

Dick and Ann Abel have been a huge part of my life. I have told my kids of the man who was responsible for my becoming a Christian back in 1971. Dick and Ann call me when they are in Colorado, and we have lunch or breakfast and catch up on what the Lord has been doing in our lives. Dick has been the biggest influence in my life toward the Lord. He showed me that being a Christian is something I don't have to hide. He showed me I can make a difference for good for those around me. Dick's legacy to me is to follow his example in that I too can be an influence for good, for those around me. I can accomplish anything that the Lord lays out for me to do. I just need to trust that what He has sent me to do. He has provided the means to accomplish it. I love Dick Abel, the man. My desire is to have similar impact on those around me.

Don(nie) DeLair—One more of our Boys

It all comes back to me. The year was 1975, and I hear that raspy voice of Dick Abel saying, "DeLair, we are starting an FCA group...at your house, and you're the president." General Abel, or Colonel Abel as he was known back then, saw something in me that my own dad didn't see. Or if he did, he didn't know how to appropriately challenge me in those areas. When no one showed up for that meeting, I felt like I had let Colonel Abel down. He asked me, "Did you do your best?"

I answered through tears, "Ye-ye-yes, sir."

"Well, that is all that matters," he said. Then we went outside to shoot some hoops.

That summer, the general found a way to send me to an FCA camp at Pt. Loma University, where I gave my life to the Lord. I have been involved with FCA ever since in a variety of capacities, and my wife and I send one child to FCA camp every summer.

I am now entering my twenty-sixth year as headmaster, the last twenty spent at King's Schools in Palm Springs—a ministry that God called me start. So much of who I am today and my ministry is credited to the grace of God, of course, and how He used General Abel to change my life for eternity.

I should have said these things years ago. Thank you, General Abel. Someday when we're both in glory with Jesus, I will be among a large group of men and women who will be standing in line to say, "It was worth it. Thank you, General Abel and Ann, for believing, investing, and challenging me to live life in the light of eternity."

Now, in the immortal words of the man who actually beat me in basketball that night so long ago in Honolulu, "Put on your barbed-wire jockstrap and get back to work!"

I love you, Dick Abel.

*Personal Note: Of the twelve original Radford high school FCA members, three went to the Air Force Academy, two to the Naval Academy and on to West Point. Unfortunately, Colonel Gary Lorenzen and Navy Lieutenant Commander Andy died while serving our nation. Several of the boys are now in full-time Christian ministry.

Karen Trimble

Senior Executive Assistant for the Military Ministry

I met Dick and Ann Abel when I came to serve at the headquarters of Campus Crusade's Military Ministry in Newport News, Virginia, as his Executive Assistant in August 2000. General Abel was a great teacher or "coach" as many often called him. I came to the ministry with a steep learning curve before me and he showed such patience as I continued to develop my skills. When you are an executive assistant, you look forward to the day when you understand the "commander's intent" (military term) and can operate in such a way that you have their complete trust, which enables you to make decisions on their behalf. We reached that point in our work relationship, and it really empowered me to fully develop my capabilities as a leader.

We served together in that capacity for five years and then continued our relationship as he and Ann transitioned to serve as members of the ministry's executive committee.

Dick Abel was/is truly a *servant leader* and led his team at Military Ministry by serving. As mentioned above, General Abel was a patient teacher/coach as he lead other ministry leaders. He was decisive when making decisions, which lends a confidence to the team. He was able to *cast the vision* in such a way with his great communication skills that he was an easy leader to follow.

General Abel taught many leadership courses throughout the years we worked together, and I do remember him saying often, "You don't manage people, you lead them." Another saying that I still use to this day is his reference to operating with "rigid flexibility." Make a decision, yet be flexible enough to change if needed.

General Abel and Ann are both family oriented, and the family has really grown in the years since we first met. His children and grandchildren would often visit the office where we worked, and it was so nice to have that connection with the Abel clan. To this day, he will update me on the latest addition to the family, wedding, etc. I loved that he called Ann "Annabel" or Miss Ann, and he exhibited such respect and admiration for her.

Today, we live in the same community, and General Abel is on the executive committee of the Military Ministry of which I work with very closely. He will call often just to say hello and visit for a while.

I believe I learned most of my leadership skills from General Abel. Communication with your team is so important. He demonstrated how encouragement and affirmation, genuine interest in staff members and their families, real love and compassion for people is so important. He exhibited grace and forgiveness when I needed it most. As a leader in the ministry now, I use all of these attributes to lead my team.

General Abel is loved by so many because he loved them first. In this he modeled Jesus to each of us. Although he could be firm at times, he always encouraged the best in others and was really an amazing *life coach* to help each of us achieve our goals. When General Abel enters the room, you always hear him before you see him, and it always brings a smile to my face. I've heard him called, "Bigger than Life Abel." The General does have a bigger than life personality yet remains a humble servant of the Lord.

Dr. Jim Cook

Pastor of the International Baptist Church in Honolulu, Hawaii, where our family attended for six years while living in Hawaii

Our relationship with Dick started many years ago when we were ministering in Hawaii and they were assigned there where he served on Admiral McCain's staff. A relationship started on a very slow pace because of people having told Dick about me as pastor, and there was a hesitation, but that didn't last long.

When I first met Dick, I was taken by his gift of communication. Right from the very start, I realized that he had an unusual gift and that was manifested in the assignments he had up to this point in the Air Force and for the rest of his career. There was an inquisitiveness about the things of the Lord that I perceived and the Lord used that contact for me to be able to follow up and make sure that he had the assurance of salvation. Soon after, I had the privilege of baptizing him in the ocean in Hawaii. There were people all around us when I asked, "Dick, have you put your trust in Jesus Christ?"

In his strong voice, he answered, "Without a doubt I have."

I asked then, "Would you like to be baptized?"

"Yes, yes, I would," he answered again strongly, clearly.

That was the beginning of a tremendous relationship that we have had all through these many years since.

Dick and Ann made a wonderful team as they worked together with the youth in Foster Village, Hawaii. Many that came to Christ in the Bible studies they conducted came forward in the church to declare their faith and were baptized, and may I add that a number went into full-time work for the Lord Jesus. Dick and Ann became staunch followers of the Lord Jesus and supporters of the body of Christ at International Baptist Church. His ability with people was manifested in many ways in his work in Hawaii and also later in the Pentagon. Some of the unique memories I have of Dick we're related to ministry outreaches. He made arrangements for me to speak many times at military functions including the Air War College and on several occasions in the Pentagon.

There was a certain period when I was in great difficulty at the church I was pastoring. In fact, I was ready to resign. In a cabin on an overnight trip, I explained the problems to Dick when he made a statement that has stayed with me. He said, "Well, at Command when we assign an officer, we don't ask him to be happy, but we tell him to fix the problem." He then pointed his finger at me and added, "General, go and fix the problem."

Thank God I did, and I am eternally grateful that I remained at the church, and the Lord gave us tremendous victory and a new determination. I have cherished the relationship for decades of years with this man, Dick Abel. We are like brothers with high respect for each other for which I praise the Lord.

Our families have had the privilege of staying close to each other over the years as the children grew up and subsequently have established themselves across the country. On numerous occasions, we have spent vacations together, shared speaking engagements, and ministered together. We became uncle and auntie to their family, and they to ours. The ministry and ongoing friendship is unique, and we treasure the great fellowship with the Abel family.

It is interesting how our leadership roles in different areas as in so many points are alike. He has become one of my most trusted friends, and I consider him as one of the great gifts God gave to me as we continue to minister around the world and across the nation.

The legacy of Richard Abel will be one of the most productive Christian leaders in this nation. He's had the privilege, because of his background at the academy and in athletics, to minister to many coaches and athletes across the country. Regarding his military career, he is the most effective Christian General during and after retirement that I have ever known. I want those reading this book to remember Dick Abel as a servant of the Lord Jesus Christ, uniquely gifted by the Lord and that gifting he has used to be productive in his Christian walk. The story of his life should inspire us all to greater depths and higher heights in Christ.

Hal Smarkola

Special Assistant (aide) while at the Pentagon

In March 1979, I received orders from the Air Force Military Personnel Center to report to the Pentagon, to SAF/OI (I believe that's what it was called at that time), and to work in the Civil Affairs Branch, Community Relations, in the old area, 4A120, a beautiful location in the Pentagon, no windows in the entire section, and right above the cafeteria on the third floor, so the smells were horrible! At that time, General Dick Abel was the Special Assistant to the Chairman Joint Chiefs of Staff, General Vessey. During my time as a captain/action officer, I had several opportunities to coordinate some of my staff summary sheets with General Abel in his office in the chairman's office. My first impression was, "Man, this guy has it all together." I could tell in an instant that he was a leader, basically a one person Public

Affairs (PA) shop! I mean, his demeanor was that of a fighter pilot, the way he stood up so straight, now a PA for the chairman of the Joint Chiefs, a former football player, his command voice, his smile, his sense of humor. Everything about him caught my attention!

General Abel was sharp, athletic, had charisma, talked football, yet he was totally *listening* to what I was saying and truly wanted to help me. He was genuine and sincere. And all that came from my first meeting with the man.

General Abel was selected as the director of public affairs in August of 1980. Again, I was gently tucked away in SAF/OICC, as a happy little action officer, keeping my nose out of trouble. But I was totally familiar with General Abel and the opinion I had already formed of him, so when he was named our boss, I was ecstatic.

When General Abel's special assistant left, I was in line for the job, but I didn't think I would get the appointment but was very excited at the prospect of working with General Abel. He spoke to me privately and said, "You've really done well. You are what I'm looking for."

I can remember exactly what I said, "Sir, before you have a chance to change your mind, and I don't know if this is even where you're going, but if you're offering me the job to be your special assistant, I don't need any time to think about it, I'll be there tomorrow morning!"

The General and I even carpooled to and from the office over the next three years. In this time, my wife and I actually became part of the Abel family, and they became a part of ours. It was incredible and beautiful to watch it happen. Our lives were changed forever.

The hours were long, the work was tough, but General Abel had the charisma, the leadership qualities that made it fun to come to work. He made it rewarding, and he took care of his people—a true caring, genuine person who believed in what he was doing, and he earned the respect of those who worked for him so that they believed too. As a respected, loved leader of the PA career field, he was in his own unique category.

I lived in Chantilly, Virginia, out Route 50, and General Abel and his family lived in Annandale, just off Little River Turnpike and Route 236. This was my morning regimen. I woke each morning at 0430, left my house by 0500 or 0515, or so, to be at the Abel's house by 0545. I would see the family in their bathrobes, fresh out of bed, dragging to the breakfast table, sharing a morning spiritual session, and then the General and I would be on the road to the Pentagon by 0600. I mean, you can't get much closer to a family than that. General Abel and I would pick up two "slugs" (slang for two people standing at the bus stop on Little River Turnpike waiting for a bus to the Pentagon) so that we could then use the carpool lane, which meant all the difference in the world in getting into the Pentagon. We would arrive in time for General Abel to hold a staff meeting of his division chiefs at 0630 so that he could be prepared for his 0700 meetings first with the chief of staff (General Lew Allen) and his staff and then the secretary of the Air Force (Mr. Verne Orr) and his staff.

On the drive in, I would be behind the wheel as General Abel was already in full work mode giving me directions for the day. My plate was full by the time I got to work. While I was driving, I would quickly learn to master the technique of word association to help remember the assigned tasks that day. We were busy nonstop all day with meetings, trip plans, conferences, letters, and general communication. Then, around 1800 each evening, we would start to think about heading home. But that's when everything would break loose from the folks on the west coast/Texas, etc. So usually, we would be lucky to get out by 1900/1930. We would get to his home about 1930/2000, and I would get home about 2000/2030, ready to eat, watch the news, and go to bed and start again the next morning. It was tough work, but it was fun. General Abel's personality, his loyalty to his senior leaders, to the Air Force, to his family, and to me and his staff and everyone who worked for him made it easy to put in those hours.

He was sincere, believed in us, believed in the Air Force, its leaders, and he was sympathetic. But he was also demanding and free to give praise for a job well done. In short, he was a caring, charismatic leader. Everyone who met General Abel reacted the same way. He commanded respect and loyalty and earned it, not because of his outer facade but because of his inner being. The firm handshake, the smile, the way he looked you in the eye, his military bearing, all told you he was ready to listen to you and respond.

The people who worked with General Abel flourished as we literally saw him taking care of us, imbedding action officers as "horse holders" (additional duty to provide public affairs assistance to air staff directors). He meant what he said he was going to do, and he did it, and no way would we ever have let that man down after seeing him go out on a limb for us time after time. He earned our respect and loyalty. If you consider where all those folks are today, how successful they were in their military careers and where they are in their civilian careers, it is clear that the time with General Abel was life changing for all of them.

Outside the military lifestyle, Ann was just a wonderful, loving lady with a heart as big as the world. She was a blessing and a totally supportive wife of not only the military but of the entire PA team. The Abels were a genuine, wonderful family. I got to know the children like members of my own family, and it was just great watching them grow up. And everything, I mean everything, was guided by General Abel's and Ann's devotion to our Lord and Savior. Christ was ever present in their lives.

General Abel was responsible for developing an organization that focused on leadership training for young officers. To this day, my fellow members of the Young Captain's Protective Society are as strong as ever, even as we're in our sixties and seventies!

It was an example of empowering young officers, and then they led by example. That's what General Abel set up, and it didn't happen accidentally nor by magic. It happened with the stroke of that man's pen and his forward-thinking mind! That's what a leader does.

I've never seen a better example of leadership in action. Our action officers were the envy of every other service. The Marines, for example, came and asked General Abel to let our action officers work with them to set up a media training program because they had none. The marines still have a great media training program in effect.

General Abel also instituted a program called the "Distinguished Civic Leader's Dinner" program where we took maybe three or four senior Air Force generals to a city with very little military presence. These men were able to meet and network with the senior leaders of that city. The program had outstanding results and again was the envy of the other services.

No one could argue that the hours were long, the work was extremely difficult, but General Abel put some fun in the program with events like the staff picnic, the golf tournament, biweekly softball games, and the Christmas Front Office party. There were plenty of opportunities to have a good time and our people did.

The general also made groundbreaking connections as he reached out to the professional athletic teams in the area as we constantly worked projects with Joe Gibbs and the Redskins and Tom Landry/Roger Staubach with the Dallas Cowboys, to name a few.

There were two especially touching moments I remember sharing with General Abel. The first occurred when I was selected for promotion to the first field grade rank, Major. This is a very significant promotion/grade in the Air Force and the person who told me I was on the list was General Abel. He also told me I was on the in-residence schools list, which meant that I would be going to Air Command and Staff College in residence at Maxwell

Air Force Base in Alabama. I was driving to Andrews Air Force Base from the Pentagon at the time of the call as I was setting up some meetings for the general. Anyway, he personally called me at the Andrews O Club to tell me the news. I was singing all the way back to the Pentagon! It was quite a feeling. Then, the best part came later when General Abel did me the honor of pinning the gold oak leaf clusters on for me. It was a special point in my life when my wife, my sister, my mom and dad, and several good friends were able to attend the ceremony and meet General Abel and Ann. It was a special point in my parents' lives too. They were working class folks from a small town outside of Philadelphia getting to meet a general in the Air Force—a caring, charismatic, genuine type of general. They loved it.

Another meaningful moment for me is when Ann asked me if I would consider planning a very special birthday celebration for General Abel on his fiftieth birthday in 1983. That was a no brainer. "Of course I'll set it up," I said. With the help of my fellow PA action officer, Bud Rothgeb, who was just an incredible comedian, we pulled it off, and it was absolutely awesome! It was one of the best events I've ever worked, full of fun, tears, hugs, relatives, videos, songs, vocalists, we had it all. I know it was especially touching for General Abel, Ann, and his family.

We stay in constant contact via e-mail and see each other on several occasions throughout the years. My wife and I became an extension of the Abel family, and what a wonderful family it is. When we celebrated the one hundredth birthday for Ann's mom here in San Antonio, we were able to see the entire family once again, but now they were all grown up and successful. I didn't know how significantly my life would change through my relationship with General Abel. His influence, encouragement, and unwavering faith had a profound impact upon me and my wife. Knowing the Abel family has been an absolute blessing. This bond is forever.

Karen Hughes Ward

Niece

I have thought about and written many wonderful things about my uncle Dick Abel but have tried to condense my thoughts, and I admit this is not an easy task! Do I say first and foremost, that it is because of him that I discovered a relationship with Jesus Christ, the most significant thing in my life? Do I tell the reader that Uncle Dick's daily teachings include this most basic principle, "If you have nothing good to say about someone, just say nothing"?

Do I include the fact that Dick Abel's work exemplifies T-E-A-M; it is all about TEAM? He taught me that if you sincerely care about the people around you, no one will ever accuse you of self-aggrandizing decisions. He also taught me that it is important to "keep a position of rigid flexibility," a mantra that I have used in my personal and professional life for over thirty years because "A good plan is always capable of revision when it is a TEAM decision."

Uncle Dick really puts the needs of others before his own but simultaneously is able to get the job done—not always so easy.

In short, my uncle Dick is an honorable man who has taught me the value of God, family and country as no one else ever could. Why? Because he *walks* his *talk* every day.

I am grateful for the opportunity to publicly praise my uncle for all he has meant to me in my life. He loves me in spite of myself and is my only real father figure. I am so grateful it was he who was the inspiration for many of the governing values in my personal and professional life. It is just a shame that the impetuousness of youth made this realization come so late in my life! With a grateful heart for all he has done in my life and in the lives of countless others, I know his impact will last for generations to come.

Ben Manthei

Successful business owner and board member for Crusade for Christ

I first met General Dick Abel through another business friend. In the early nineties, we attended an event called Vision Weekend sponsored by the Military Ministry of Campus Crusade for Christ (CCC). As General Abel finished speaking, he challenged us to pray for the Military Ministry of CCC. I had already began praying daily as I walked to the lake near our home and back. I first learned about "prayer walking" at a Promise Keepers meeting and enjoyed spending that time in prayer. I added General Abel to my list and prayed for him and the ministry every working day for an entire year.

When I saw him again, the following year, I introduced myself and said, "General Abel, I have prayed for you every day since we met."

That immediately got his attention. He was so very grateful.

At that second meeting, he not only asked us to pray, but he challenged us to get involved financially with the ministry. We have multiple businesses, and we are continually asked to donate or give to various causes, and I was not looking to give to another ministry but was drawn to consider it.

"I tell you what," I told General Abel privately. "You work with military guys, right? Well, I have a niece who is married to a young man in the navy, but their marriage is in trouble. Could you reach out to them, see what you can do for their relationship?"

Four months later I received a call. It was the general. "Hi, Ben. Listen, I have someone here who wants to talk to you." Then he hands the phone to someone, and the next voice I hear belongs to my niece's husband. He explained how he had prayed to receive Christ and how the decision had changed their marriage and their lives forever. That event helped form our enduring friendship. The general asked us to serve on the board of advisors for the Military Ministry, a position held for twelve years.

Many years ago, General Abel asked me to call him Dick. I just couldn't do it, still can't. I am most comfortable with calling him Coach. And Coach cares about people. That is the basic, driving force of his life, to care and love people. When you are in his presence, he makes you feel like you are the only guys in the room.

Coach invited me along on mission trips for the international military ministry. We probably visited a half a dozen countries, visiting ships at sea and military bases around the world. I learned so much from him through those years. He is one of the top three mentors in my life, and I am blessed to know him. Of course, we learned to know and love Annie too as we traveled together.

Coach stretched me beyond my comfort zone when he would ask me to speak and share my testimony on those trips. I didn't know I could do that, but God blessed me, and we had phenomenal results.

He challenged me to speak more and then report back to him with the outcome. He was convinced that leaders who know how to communicate through the spoken and written word will always be successful. He also taught me that leadership is about people. "You lead people, you manage assets," he told me. "And the way you lead people is by loving them and serving them."

Favorite memories include speaking at Kenya's military base and sharing at a Moscow missile base and impacting the Russian general of that base. I will always find it humorous that Coach could fly super powerful fighter jets, but he had a problem managing a snowmobile. Nearly every time he hopped on one, he ended up rolling down the mountain after tipping the thing over. Reminds me of one of Coach's favorite sayings: Kick the tires and light the fires 'cause he has a need for speed. Funny.

One principle I learned from Coach is this: Cool down when you're angry or want to lash out at or strike back at someone.

He learned through the years to listen, yes, even to your critics and then reply calmly, "Let me process that." I have applied that advice many times in business.

I appreciate Coach as a family man too. I know he treasures his wife and children.

When thinking about Coach's legacy I believe people will say he was a general's general that loved people. He was a leader that loved people, and people loved him. He led out of relationship—not fear, not needs, but out of relationship. And he will be remembered for his deep faith; everything was about sharing his faith with others. He was twenty years older but reached back to someone like me, pulled me up, and now I've learned to reach back and pull others along too. Thanks, Coach.

George Toles

Businessman and Friend

My wife, Liz, and I met Dick and Ann at a Pro Athletes Outreach conference years ago. It was bosom buddies at first sight. You couldn't help but notice and appreciate the leadership skills he exhibited, his strengths, how he worked with others, the general feelings of those who worked with or for him.

Dick is always in focus, outcome-oriented, amazingly humble despite all of his celebrated accomplishments, and owns an unsinkable sense of humor and smile. He is fearless in his faith, firmly committed to living for Christ.

Once about five years ago Dick and I were having lunch at a Mexican restaurant in Bothell, Washington, near his daughter's home in Seattle. Realizing that he had so much wisdom and experience to share, we brainstormed how he could develop a speaking and writing career. I introduced him to the idea of blogging to build a loyal following of potential readers, conference leaders, and personal appearance schedulers. We drilled down into what the message of his life is, deciding that it was to help leaders stay on the right path. "Vector Corrector" seemed like the perfect description for an Air Force pilot and a great title for a book. Glad to see that come to fruition.

We're still in weekly contact via e-mail and speak several times a year by phone, and we see Dick and Ann whenever they come to Seattle for family visits. I value his friendship very much. Dick is a man's man, military hero, loyal to his country and to others, driven to spread God's love and Good News, a servant to his family, is so approachable, plugged into an impressive network, and always ready to offer his assistance.

Dick reminds me of Winston Churchill, a "never give up, never retire, full out" brother in Christ and friend. He's proven that no matter how impressive your position in rank and in life, you're never too busy or too important to give first place to being available to answer God's call with an energetic "All present and accounted for, sir!" I'm blessed to call him friend.